Celebrity Cameos

Seventy-one Mini Biographies
from the Golden Age
of Cinema and Music

by
M. Dee Dubroff

Introduction

This treasure trove of little known facts about some of the world's most famous actors and musicians is both informative and fascinating. Here you can find tidbits about your favorite stars of stage and screen, which in their humanity makes them close to the real world. So have fun on this magical carpet ride into the stardust of yesteryear.

Dedication

This compendium is dedicated
to lovers of the golden age of cinema.

Contents

Alan Ladd:
A Drinking Life
(1913-1964)

Alan Walbridge Ladd was born in Hot Springs, Arkansas on September 3, 1913. He was the only child of Ina Raleigh (aka Selina Rowley) and Alan Ladd, a freelance accountant. His mother was English, hailing from County Durham, and his paternal grandparents were Canadian. His mother emigrated to the United States at the age of 19, and his father died when Alan was only four years old.

At the age of five, while playing with matches, he set fire to the family home, and his mother moved with Alan to Oklahoma City. There she met and married a house painter, and they moved again when Alan was eight, this time to California. At a very early age, Alan began working at odd jobs such as: picking fruit, delivering newspapers and sweeping floors.

He discovered track and swimming in high school, and by 1931 was training for the 1932 Olympics. An accidental injury closed the door on that particular dream. In 1936, he married his friend, Midge, and they had one son, Alan Ladd, Jr. At one point, his destitute mother moved in with the couple, and a few months later she committed suicide by ingesting ant poison in front of Alan! He and Midge divorced, and in 1939, talent scout, Sue Carol, is credited with discovering him. They later married.

Alan Ladd was known for his small stature and indifferent affect. He became a star after his performance as a hit man with a conscience in *This Gun For Hire (1942)*. Perhaps his most famous role is that of a gunfighter in the film, *Shane* (1953). He made seven films with Veronica Lake, who was his favorite co-star because she was a petite woman and made him seem taller than his five foot, five inch frame. Their films together included: *The Glass Key* (1942), *Star Spangled Rhythm* (1942), *This Gun For Hire* (1942), *Duffy's Tavern*, (1945), *The Blue Dahlia* (1946), *Saigon* (1948), and *Variety Girl* (1947).

In a 1961 interview, Ladd was asked, "What would you change about yourself if you could?" He replied: "Everything." On January 29, 1964, at the age of 50, he was found dead from an accidental overdose of alcohol and sedatives. He left three children (two sons and one daughter) and a legacy of many fine films.

Source: https://www.imdb.com / name/nm0000042/bio
Image: 5 Minute Biographies.com

Alfred Hitchcock:
The Master of
Terror and Suspense
(1899-1980)

Is there any one in the world who has not seen and shivered at the shower scene in the classic film, *Psycho*? What made the films of Alfred Hitchcock so very special? Read on for some thoughts, and perhaps a few shivers as well.

To this very day, I never get into the shower without a momentary flashback to that famous scene. I even keep the edges of my shower curtain open a little bit, almost as if to prepare myself for the sight of Norman Bates approaching. The impact of that movie has receded over time, but it has never left my memory.

The short, pudgy, dour-faced Englishman, who always looked as if he had just swallowed a lemon, was a genius like no other. In an interview shortly before his death in 1980, he was asked why the iconic shower scene was not filmed in color. He replied without a moment's hesitation: "That would have been in bad taste. and black and white was much more connected to the symbolism of Janet Leigh's life slipping down the drain." That is the response of a true artist.

So many tried to imitate his style and none could even come close. All they gleaned from *Psycho* was a knife in the hands of a lunatic, and the film was so much more than that.

In Leytonstone, Essex, England in 1899, Alfred Joseph was the youngest of three children born to a Roman Catholic green grocer. He described himself as a well-behaved boy who could not recall ever playing with other children. One of his favorite stories was about his father sending him to the local police station with a note when he was five; the policeman looked at the note and locked him in a cell for a few minutes, saying, "This is what we do to naughty boys." The experience left him, with a lifelong fear of wrongful conviction and policemen, two themes that are often present in his films. (*The Wrong Man, 1956*)

His early films held a particular fascination as well. They were often cinematic tales of espionage and mistaken identities and ladies vanishing all across the English countryside (*The Lady Vanishes, 1938).*

He said his own personal favorite was *Shadow of a Doubt*, which was made in in 1943 and starred Joseph Cotton, Theresa Wright and Patricia Collinge. The story of a prodigal uncle with a homicidal past is fascinating fare for lovers of the *film noir* genre, and Joseph Cotton is superb as a woman-hating psychopath.

To this day, Hitchcock's films are durable masterpieces that are well worth viewing for an optimum cinematic experience.

His television show, *Alfred Hitchcock Presents*, which aired in the 1950s, was extraordinary for its time, and many a famous star can be seen in these half-hour vignettes of terror and suspense. The music for the show, his theme song so-to-speak, was part of an old English funeral march, and he cleverly began each show by stepping into the caricature of his own profile (which he himself drew, by the way). His wit always came to the surface in his announcements both before and after each presentation. He died in 1980 and left legacy of many fine films.

Source: https://www.biography.com / people/alfred-hitchcock-9340006
Photo by Pierre Vauthey / Sygma/Sygma via Getty Images

Ann Bancroft: An Actress of Distinction (1931-2005)

Anna Maria Italiano was born to Italian-American parents on September 17, 1931, in The Bronx, New York. A graduate of the American Academy of Dramatic Arts in Manhattan, she made her cinematic debut in 1952 in *Don't Bother To Knock*. At this time, Twentieth Century Fox thought her real name to be too ethnic for the cinema. Out of all the names offered, she opted for Bancroft because she thought it sounded "like a dignified name." Her skill as an actress was quickly recognized by the powers-that-be, and she made many films as a supporting actress during the 1950s.

She said Arthur Penn was the person who had the greatest impact on her career. He directed the film which made her a star in 1962. For her performance in *The Miracle Worker* she won an Academy Award and went on to other memorable starring roles.

The 1960s were her most prolific decade. Some of her films of note include: *The Pumpkin Eater,* which co-starred Peter Finch and was directed by Jack Clayton (1964), *Seven Women* (1966), which was directed by John Ford, and Mike Nichol's *The Graduate* (1967). In her role as the seductress of a much younger man in *The Graduate*, she was really only six years older than co-star, Dustin Hoffman. In the years that followed, many young men told her that she was their first sexual fantasy.

She and her husband, Mel Brooks, met on the set of a talk show and later Mel bribed one of the workers on the show to tell him which restaurant Ann would be dining in that evening so that he could "accidentally" run into her. They married in August of 1964 and were together for more than forty years (until her death). They had one son, Max, born in 1972. As the story goes, they married at New York's City Hall, where a stranger who happened to be passing by served as their witness. A Catholic by birth, Ann converted to Judaism after marrying Brooks.

For her work in television, she received a star on the Hollywood Walk of Fame on Hollywood Boulevard. With her passing on June 6, 2005 of uterine cancer, the world lost a uniquely gifted actress. She left a formidable roster of many fine films.

Source: https://www.imdb.com / name/nm0000843
Image: Pinterest

**Audrey Hepburn:
A More Than Fair Lady
(1929-1993)**

Born on May 4, 1929,
Audrey Kathleen Ruston
began her life in Brussels,
Belgium. She was the only
child of an Anglo-Irish
banker, Joseph Anthony
Ruston, and Baroness Ella
van Heemstra, a Dutch
aristocrat who was
descended from French and English kings.
Her father later added the name Hepburn to his surname,
making her Audrey Hepburn-Ruston. She had two half-brothers,
Alexander and Ian Quarles, by her mother's first marriage to a
Dutch nobleman.

As a child, Audrey attended private schools in England and The
Netherlands. Her life was a bubble until her parents divorced in
1935, and she went with her mother to live in The Netherlands
during the Nazi invasion and occupation of Holland. Here, she
saw and experienced hunger and deprivation for the first time in
her sheltered life. She suffered from malnutrition and sustained
health problems that plagued her for the rest of her life. She joined
a ballet group and collected money for the underground movement.
The impact of these terrible times would never leave her mind and
shaped her life and her values.

After the war, she moved with her mother to London where she
studied ballet. In 1951, after appearing in a few films, she was
offered the leading role in the Broadway play, *Gigi*. Soon after, real

stardom came with a leading role opposite Gregory Peck in *Roman Holiday*(1953).

Even though she was not yet a star, Peck insisted she share top billing with him. For this role, she won the 1953 Academy Award for Best Actress and became a star in her own right.

Sabrina followed in 1954, and then in 1961 the role that made her a cultural icon, Holly GoLightly, in *Breakfast at Tiffany's*.

She was a spokesperson for UNICEF and a great humanitarian. She died of cancer on January 20, 1993 at the age of 64, leaving two sons and her beloved significant other, Dutch businessman Robert Wolder, who was 25 years her junior, not to mention a world of adoring fans. Her career spanned more than three decades and almost thirty films.

Source: https://www.imdb.com / name/nm0000030/bio
Photo by Hulton Archive / Getty Images

Barbara Stanwyck: She Who Never Won An Oscar (1907-1990)

Born Ruby Catherine Stevens in Brooklyn, New York, on July 17, 1907, Barbara Stanwyck has often been dubbed "the best actress who never won an Oscar." A theatrical poster that read: Jane Stanwyck starring in *Barbara Freitchie* inspired her stage name. Her parents, Byron and Catherine McGee Stevens, were poor Scots-Irish immigrants, and Barbara and her siblings (Maude, Mabel, Mildred and Malcolm Byron) became motherless when she was only four, after her mother was accidentally pushed off a trolley car by a drunk and killed. Soon after, her father abandoned the entire family.

She graduated from Erasmus Hall High and took a job at the local phone company for $14 a week to help support herself and her four siblings. When not working, she pounded the pavement in search of dancing jobs and soon she was hired as a chorus girl at the age of 17 and was earning $40 dollars a week. She also worked briefly as a fashion model in the late 1920s.

She moved to Hollywood in 1928 and soon began one of the most lucrative careers the world of cinema has ever seen. She was very versatile and appeared in comedies, melodramas and westerns. One of her best films, *Double Indemnity*, in which she starred opposite Fred MacMurray, was made in 1944.

She was a hard working actress who always performed to the best of her ability, and she was considered very easy-going and a pleasure to work with.

She did much work in television as well, notably as the matriarch, Victoria Barclay, of *The Big Valley* (1965). She also starred in the hit mini-series, *The Thorn Birds*, in 1983. She died on January 20, 1990.

Her career spanned almost six decades and she appeared in 93 movies.

Source: https://www.imdb.com/name/nm0001766/bio
Photo via John Kobal Foundation / Getty Images

Bette Davis:
Actress Extraordinaire
(1908-1989)

Surely there are few cinematic faces more recognizable than that of the dark haired, seductive *First Lady of The American Screen*, Betty Davis. Those large brown eyes, immortalized in the 1980s pop song, *Bette Davis Eyes*, are seen throughout the world every day of the year even though she has been gone for more than three decades. Her film credits are many, totaling more than 100 in her lifetime, and her performances remain sterling and durable even with the passage of more than half a century.

Ruth Elizabeth Davis was born in Lowell, Massachusetts, on April 5, 1908. Her mother was an aspiring actress who encouraged Bette in every way, while her stern, disdainful father, Harlow, did little to foster his daughter's dreams. He left the family before she reached her tenth birthday and her mother, Ruthie, sent Bette and her sister to boarding school. After graduation, she enrolled in dramatic school in 1929, and made her Broadway debut in *Broken Dishes*. She then moved to Hollywood to screen test for Universal and the rest is history.

Although she earned a reputation as being difficult to work with, there is no question that Bette Davis stood up to and tweaked the powers-that-be in the Hollywood of her day. Her attitude set a precedent for women. Even though she had signed a contract with Warner's, she was unhappy with the roles offered to her. She challenged the studio by going to London to make movies. Jack

Warner sued her for breach of contract and she was forced to return and honor it, but when she did, she was offered a new contract and better roles.

Bette Davis was the first Warner Brother's actress to win an Academy Award for her role in *Dangerous* in 1935. Another followed for *Jezebel* in 1938, and all in all, she received eight Academy Award nominations. Her proudest personal achievement was her aid to the war effort by helping to organize the Hollywood Canteen during World War II for soldiers passing through Los Angeles.

Her film career spanned more than fifty years and included such classics as: *The Petrified Forest (1936)*, *Dark Victory(1939)*, *All The Little Foxes (1941)*, *Now, Voyageur* (1942), *Watch on The Rhine (1943)*, *A Stolen Life (1946)*, *All About Eve* (1950) *Whatever Happened to Baby Jane (1962)*, *Dead Ringer(1964)* *The Nanny* (1965) and too many others to reiterate here.

She was a star of immense proportions and a woman of courage, integrity, purpose and talent. Married four times, she had one daughter with her third husband, William Grant Sherry, and adopted two others, Margot and Michael, while married to Gary Merrill, her fourth and final husband. She died in France on October 6, 1989 at the age of 81.

Source: https://www.biography.com/people/bette-davis-9267626
Photo Source: Getty Images

Betty Grable:
Million Dollar Legs
(1918-1973)

Born on December 18, 1916, in St.Louis, Missouri, Elizabeth Ruth Grable was the daughter of German and Dutch immigrants, John C. Grable and Lillian Hoffman. Her mother was materialistic and determined that her daughter would become a star. She enrolled Elizabeth, later known as Betty, in dancing school when she was only three years of age. Under her mother's guidance, she studied ballet and tap dancing. At 13, she and her mother set out for Hollywood with high hopes of stardom and fame.

Lying about her daughter's age landed Betty several parts in minor films, her first as a chorus girl in the film, *Happy Days* (1929). Her age was difficult to determine because for this particular part she performed in black face in a chorus line, but with closer examination came a fake ID, for which Betty got fired. But Betty (or perhaps Lillian) wouldn't give up, and Betty soon became a 'Goldwyn Girl' in the film, *Whoopee*. Betty Grable was in fact one of the original 'Goldwyn Girls' along with Lucille Ball, Virginia Bruce, Ann Dvorak and Paulette Goddard.

By 1939, Betty had played in some twenty films, including Academy Award nominated *The Gay Divorcee*, starring Fred Astaire and Ginger Rogers. In 1937, she married former child actor, Jackie Coogan, but the couple divorced in 1940. That same year, Betty obtained a contract with Twentieth Century Fox and soon became their top star. It was during this time that she posed for her famous pin-up photo, which soon became a symbol of escapism for American GIs stationed overseas in World War II. This poster was featured in the iconic war film, *Stalag 17.*

Betty dated both Desi Arnaz and George Raft, which ended after two years because Raft could not get a divorce from his Catholic wife. She starred in *Down Argentine Way (1940), MoonOver Miami (1941), I Wake Up Screaming (1941) Springtime in The Rockies (1942), Coney Island (1943),* and *Pin Up Girl (1944),* In the late 1940s, Fox studio insured her legs with Lloyds of London for a quarter million dollars!

She married musician, Harry James in 1943, and the couple, who divorced in 1965, had two daughters, Victoria and Jessica. She lived a life that was full, happy and without scandal.

She died of lung cancer at the too young age of 56 on July 2, 1973.

Source: https://en.wikipedia.org/wiki/Betty_Grable
Photo by Silver Screen Collection / Getty Images

Billy Holiday:
Tormented Talent Supreme
(1915-1959)

Eleanora Fagan, aka Lady Day, aka Billy Holiday, was born in Philadelphia, PA, on April 7, 1915, to thirteen-year-old Sadie Fagan and fifteen-year-old Clarence Holiday, a jazz guitarist for Fletcher Henderson's band. She had a troubled childhood spent in the Fellis Point section of Baltimore, Maryland, almost all of which is clouded by conjecture and legend propagated even by herself in her autobiography, which was published in 1956.

Her parents married when she was three years of age, but soon divorced, and her mother and other relatives raised her. Although Clarence Holiday accepted paternity, he was not a responsible father. Whenever she did see him, she would demand money, threatening to reveal to his then-girlfriend that he had a daughter. She was an angry child and dropped out of school at a very early age to work as a prostitute with her mother. Sometime in the 1930s, she and her mother moved to New York for a fresh start.

She settled in Harlem, and in 1932 was discovered by record producer, John Hammond, at a club called *Monette's*. He arranged for her very first recording session with none other than Benny Goodman, and the result was *Her Mother's Son-In-Law* (1933).

On November 4, 1934, she had her first success as a dancer, appearing at the Apollo Theater to glowing reviews with pianist and then lover, Bobby Henderson.

Billie performed regularly at numerous clubs on 52nd Street in Manhattan. Her voice was a unique blend of pain and torment suffused with softness and vulnerability. While on stage, she was Lady Day, singer extraordinaire, with a white gardenia pressed softly against her hair.

Her personal life was as turbulent as the songs she sang, and her success was marred by abusive relationships with men and a growing drug and alcohol dependency. She married trombonist, James Monroe, on August 25, 1941 and while still married, became the common law wife of trumpeter, Joe Guy. She divorced Monroe and later married Louis McKay who was also abusive, but he did try to get her off drugs. She never found the happiness and peace of mind she so desperately. sought.

Billie Holiday died at the age of 44 from cirrhosis of the liver on July 17, 1959. In the final years of her life, she had been swindled out of her earnings and died with 70 cents in the bank and $750 dollars on her person.

It was a terrible end for a talented but tormented Lady Day, whose music will live forever more in the hearts of her many adoring fans (this author included).

Source: https://www.biography.com/people/billie-holiday-9341902
Photo by Gilles Petard / Redferns

Boris Karloff:
The Gentle Monster
(1887-1969)

William Henry Pratt was born
on November 23, 1887 in
London, England. He was
the son of a custom's official,
John Pratt, Jr., and his third
wife, Eliza Sarah Millard. It
was originally thought that he
would pursue a diplomatic
career, and he was educated in
this field at London University.
But he changed his mind and emigrated to Canada in 1909. It
was here where both the actor and the stage name, Boris Karloff,
was born.

Along with Lon Chaney, Vincent Price and Bela Lugosi, Boris
Karloff is considered one of the true icons of the horror cinema.
His most famous role was as *Frankenstein*, based on the novel
by Mary Shelley. He toured throughout the United States and
in the early days of Hollywood, worked in silent films such as
The Deadlier Sex (1920) and *Omar, The Tentmaker* (1922). His
big break came in 1931 when he was cast as "the monster" in the
Universal production of *Frankenstein*. The director of the film,
James Whale, cleverly added to the mystery of the "monster" by
listing Karloff's name in the credits simply as " ? "

The film was a commercial success and Karloff was immediately
established as a star. He was cast in other dark roles including
The Mummy (1932) and *The Mask of Fu Manchu* (1932).

He appeared as the monster again in *The Bride of Frankenstein* with Elsa Lanchester (1935) and *The Son of Frankenstein*, (1939). This image stayed with him, and although he was very warm-hearted and affectionate towards children, when he lived in the Dakota apartments in New York back in the late 1930s, the children who lived in the same building never would 'trick or treat' at his door. It bothered him, although he understood why.

He was a wonderful actor, whose many films are still enjoyed to this day.

He died of emphysema on February 2, 1969 at the age of 82.

Source: https://www.imdb.com/name/nm0000472/bio
Photo Source: Getty Images

Burt Lancaster: The Star With The Golden Grin (1911-1994)

Born Burton Steven Lancaster, on November 2, 1911, Burt was one of the five children born to a New York City postal worker. His Irish Protestant ancestors hailed from Ulster and emigrated to The United States in the 1880s. He was a street kid who became interested in gymnastics at a very early age. This led him to the call of the circus where he worked as an acrobat until he was injured. It also gave him the great physique for which he was so well known.

As a soldier in World War II, the acting bug bit him hard. He served as a member of the Special Services Branch and he entertained American troops who were stationed with him in Italy during the war. His very first film, *The Killers* in 1946, catapulted him to stardom.

He never took an acting lesson in his life and learned his craft as he went along. In 1948, under the auspices of Harold Hecht and James Hill, he set up his own production company, the purpose of which was to direct his career. The company, Hecht-Hill-Lancaster, was responsible for many fine productions that he wasn't featured in. These included Paddy Chayefsky's *Marty* (1955) with Ernest Borgnine, who won an Oscar for his fine performance as a lonely Bronx butcher, and *The Catered Affair* with Betty Davis and Debby Reynolds in 1956.

He was known for his killer smile, which he always referred to as "the Grin." Equally proficient in Westerns, crime thrillers, comedies and drama, his friendship with Kirk Douglas was more than a bit over-rated and largely fabricated. In truth, he was often cruel to Douglas and played many practical jokes on him that were always at his expense.

An atheist and die-hard liberal, Lancaster stood up for his beliefs and was no hypocrite. He was married three times and had five children. His son, Bill Lancaster, is an actor and writer. Burt was well known as a ladies' man, and this ruined all of his marriages.

But he was very well loved as both an actor and a man. He admitted that on a movie set he was always difficult, complaining about everything and sometimes very loudly. By the end of the shoot, however, the crew was always sorry to see him go, and even he never understood why.

He died in October of 1994, leaving behind a roster of films that spanned more than forty years.

Source: https://www.imdb.com/name/nm0000044/bio
Photo by Keystone / Hulton Archive / Getty Images

Cab Calloway:
Cool And Versatile
(1907-1994)

Born December 25, 1907 in Rochester, New York, and raised primarily in Baltimore, Maryland, Cabell Calloway III began his formidable life in a middle class African-American family. His father, Cabell Calloway II, was a lawyer and his mother, Martha Eulalie Reed, was a teacher and church organist. They recognized their son's musical talent, and in 1922, gave him private voice lessons.

Throughout Cab's formative years, he studied music and voice, and despite his parents' staunch disapproval of jazz, he began frequenting and performing in many of Baltimore's jazz clubs. There he found both influence and inspiration from the likes of drummer, Chick Webb and pianist, Johnny Jones.

He learned scat singing with the help of Louis Armstrong, who tutored him before he became a regular performer at Harlem's famous *Cotton Club*. In 1931, he hit it big with what would become his signature song, *Minnie The Moocher*. It sold more than a million copies and his famous line, "hi-de-hi-de-ho" was his way of improvising when he forgot a lyric. The song was so popular that in the early 1930s his onstage moves were duplicated by animators who placed him in a few Betty Boop cartoons, and there was even one entitled: *Minnie the Moocher*.

During the 1930s and 1940s, he had many hits, which included: *Moon Glow* (1934), *The Jumpin' Jive* (1939) and *Blues in the Night* (1941). He also made numerous appearances on radio, and he was one of the most successful entertainers of the era. He appeared in several films including: *The Big Broadcast* (1932), *The Singing Kid* (1936) and *Stormy Weather* (1943).

In 1993, President Clinton presented Calloway with the National Medal of The Arts. He lived to the age of 86 and he died in 1994 in Hockessin, Delaware.

Source: https://www.biography.com/people/cab-calloway-9235609
Photo by Gilles Petard / Redferns

Cary Grant:
The British Dreamboat
(1904-1986)

When an interviewer once told Cary Grant that everybody would like to be him, he replied that "so would he." Born in Bristol, England, as Archibald Alexander Leach on January 18, 1904, his life would have been quite ordinary if his mother hadn't been placed in a mental institution when he was only nine. He was never told the truth, and he left school at age fourteen. He was largely self educated and remained a voracious reader throughout his life.

He forged his father's signature on a letter to join a group of British knockabout comedians called T*he Bob Pender Comedy Troupe.* This was his start, albeit an unlikely and shaky one. Here, he learned the art of pantomime, acrobatics and picked up a Cockney accent. He went on to tour The United States with the troupe in 1920.

He appeared in a few movies, but his big break didn't come until 1933. It was in that year that he met and fell under the tutelage and spell of Mae West, who was already an established star. It was she who single-handedly catapulted his career to stardom by choosing him as her leading man in *She Done Him Wrong.* Although Grant had appeared in movies long before this one, his comedic skill had heretofore gone unnoticed.

In 1955, he was chosen by *Empire Magazine* as one of the 100 sexiest stars in film history (Number 22, to be exact.) Due to the physical strength and dexterity he gleaned as an acrobat, Grant did many of his own stunts during his film career. He was a great fan of Elvis Presley and often attended his Las Vegas shows. His boyhood idol was Douglas Fairbanks, whose healthy tan was the inspiration for his constantly dark skin. He also maintained a year round suntan to avoid wearing makeup.

He fell madly in love with Sophia Loren when they made a film together in 1957. He still pursued her with dozens of phone calls and hundreds of flowers even when she called the affair off after becoming involved with producer, Carlo Ponti.

For the man who once said: "the only really good thing about acting is that there is no heavy lifting," his career spanned almost seventy films.

He died on November 28, 1986.

Source: https://www.biography.com/people/cary-grant-9318103
Photo Info: Creator: Herbert Dorfman Credit: Corbis via Getty Images

Charlie Chaplin: King Of the Mimes (1889-1977)

Sir Charles Spencer Chaplin, Jr. was born on April 16, 1889, in Walworth, London, England, the son of two music hall entertainers, Charles Chaplin, Sr. and Hannah Harriet Hill. His parents separated shortly after his birth, and his mother, who was unstable, became solely in charge of his care. When Charlie was twelve, his father died an alcoholic, and his mother had a nervous breakdown and was temporarily committed to a mental institution. In 1926, she went to the US to live with her successful son, dying there two years later.

He first performed in the Music Hall in 1894 at the age of five. At age eleven, in 1900, with the help of his brother, he landed the role of a comic cat in the pantomime, *Cinderella,* at the London Hippodrome. Over the next few years, he got a variety of theatrical roles, and on October 2, 1912, he came to America with the Karno Troupe. In that very same company was a man named Arthur Stanley Jefferson who would later become known as Stan Laurel. The two performers shared a room together, but Laurel soon returned to England. After seeing his act, producer Max Sennett hired Chaplin for his own studio, *The Keystone Film Company*.

He became *The Tramp* and world famous. He built his own Hollywood studio in 1918, which gave him complete creative control of all his productions. Some of his best works include:

A Dog's Life (1918), *The Kid* (1921), *The Pilgrim* (1923), *A Woman Of Paris* (1923) and *The Circus* (1928), just to name a few.

In 1919, he formed *The United Artist Film Distribution Company* with Mary Pickford, Douglas Fairbanks and D.W. Griffith and served on the board until the early 1950s. Chaplin resisted the "talkie" film all through the 1930s. A very versatile performer, he also composed the song, *Smile,* which was so beautifully recorded by Nat King Cole and others.

His first dialogue picture, *The Great Dictator* (1940) was an act of defiance against Adolph Hitler and the terrible rise of fascism. It was quite controversial and daring for its time, and it was said that the monster Hitler himself was known to have seen the film twice (information gleaned from records kept in his personal theater).

Chaplin retained his British citizenship even though he was a US resident from 1914-1952. He returned to Europe in 1952, and remained there, making his home in Vevey, Switzerland. He won two honorary Oscars, and his final film was *A Countess From Hong Kong* (1967) co-starring Sophia Loren. Personally, he had a pattern of relationships with much younger women, starting with Mildred Harris and ending with Oona O'Neil, the daughter of playwright, Eugene O'Neil, whom he married in 1943.

He fathered eleven children between 1919 and 1962. He died on Christmas Day, 1977, at the age of 88 following a stroke. In 1978, his body was stolen in an attempt to extort money from the family. Eleven weeks later, the body was recovered.

Source: https://www.imdb.com/name/nm0000122/bio
Photo by General Film Company / Getty Images

Clara Bow:
Cinema's "It" Girl
(1907-1965)

Born in a tenement in Brooklyn, New York, on July 29, 1907, Clara Bow was the only surviving daughter of a poor family afflicted with mental illness. For Clara's mother, Sarah Gordon, who worked as a prostitute, her biggest hope for Clara was that she too would die at birth, like her sisters before her. In anticipation of this, she didn't even bother getting a birth certificate!

Sarah was noted for her many affairs with local firemen and Clara's father, in the rare times when he was at home, was physically and verbally abusive to both his wife and daughter. He reportedly raped Clara when she was fifteen years old. When her father left for good, her mother turned tricks in the apartment, locking Clara up in the closet whenever a customer was there.

Sara Gordon treated her only child terribly, and one night Clara awoke to find her holding a butcher knife to her throat! As a result, she suffered from insomnia the rest of her life. Clara dropped out of school at the age of seven, and despite these horrible beginnings, by her mid-teens, she was working as an actress. Her first part was in *Beyond The Rainbow* in 1922, but to her dismay, her scenes were cut and not seen until the film was restored years later.

She became a star with the film, *The Plastic Age* (1925), which was written by feminist screenwriter, Frederica Sagor Maas. She became known for her ability to project forbidden sexuality and became the epitome of the 1920s flapper. She began to make a lot of money, and appeared in 58 motion pictures in eleven years. With wealth, she brought her father to live with her in Hollywood. She tried to set him up in several businesses, but he was as he had always been, a drunken failure. Clara always retained a humble quality, despite her fame, fortune and adoration by millions of fans.

She had numerous affairs, and all of them were fodder for the hungry tabloids of the day. In 1927, she was dubbed the "it girl", "it" being sex appeal. She went on to make the film, *Wings (1927)*, which won the first Academy Award for "Best Picture."

Her career continued with limited success into the early sound era, despite her very thick Brooklyn accent. In 1932, she married cowboy-actor, Rex Bell, and she retired from the cinema in 1933. The couple had two sons ; Tony Beldam and George Beldam, Jr.

In 1949, she was diagnosed with schizophrenia and received shock treatments. She died from a heart attack on September 27, 1965, and was given a star on the Hollywood Walk of Fame.

In 1994, she was honored with her image on a postage stamp designed by Al Hirschfeld.

Source: https://www.biography.com/people/clara-bow-9221851
Photo by Eugene Robert Richee / John Kobal Foundation / Getty Images

Clark Gable:
"Mr. Rhett, You Is Bad"
(1901-1961)

Those words were spoken by
character actress, Hattie
MacDaniel, who played
Mammy, the slave, in
Margaret Mitchell's immortal
classic about the old South,
Gone With The Wind. She said
them after receiving a red
petticoat from the notorious
Rhett Butler, a role
immortalized by Clark Gable.
Born William Clark Gable in Cadiz, Ohio, on February 1, 1901,
the King of Hollywood came from humble roots. His mother died
when he was seven, and at sixteen, he quit high school and went to
work in a tire factory in Akron.

He decided to become an actor after seeing the play, *The Bird
of Paradise*. He toured in stock companies, sold ties and toiled
in oil fields. His coach, Josephine Dillon (who was also his first
wife and seventeen years older), brought him to Hollywood. He
returned to the theater where he met and made lifelong friends with
Lionel Barrymore. He was eventually signed in 1930 in the film,
Dance, Fools Dance, and the public (particularly women) loved
him. He became an important and very popular star.

He won an Oscar for his performance in *It Happened One Night*
(1934) opposite Claudette Colbert. He also won nominations for
his portrayal of Fletcher Christian in *Mutiny On The Bounty* (1935)
and Rhett Butler in *Gone With The Wind* (1939).

Gable did not make any movies for three years following the death of his third wife, Carol Lombard, who died in a plane crash while returning from a War Bond drive in 1942. The grieving actor joined the Army Air Corps for the duration of the war. He then worked on and off for years afterwards, and died of a heart attack in 1961 at the age of 60.

It was said that his fatal attack was induced by his insistence on doing all of his own stunts in his last film, *The Misfits (1961)*.

He is buried next to his beloved, Carol Lombard.

Source: https://en.wikipedia.org/wiki/Clark_Gable
Photo: Bettmann Archive

**David Niven:
A Classic Gentleman
(1910-1983)**

Born in London, England, on March 1, 1910, James David Graham Nevins was named David after the Saint's Day on which he was born, St. David, patron saint of Wales. His father, William Edward Graham Nevins, died at the age of twenty-five during the Gallipoli Campaign in 1915, and his mother, Julia de Gacher, remarried Sir Thomas Comyn-Platt. He once wrote that as a child he felt superior to others and jokingly attributed this to the fact when reciting the Lord's Prayer in church, he could have sworn that the words were meant to read, "Our Father, who art a Niven."

As a young man, he trained at the Royal Military Academy and served two years with the Highland Light Infantry. It was here he learned the gentlemanly bearing that was to become his trademark for all of his adult life, both on and off screen.

He arrived in Hollywood during the 1930s and worked as an extra in westerns. In 1935, he got a walk-on part in *Mutiny On The Bounty*, which was quickly followed by a long-term contract with Samuel Goldwyn. This led to many starring roles for Niven, including *Bachelor Mother* (1939) with Ginger Rogers. During this time, he met and became good friends with Clark Gable. When his first wife died tragically at the age of 28 from a terrible fall at the home of Tyrone Power, it was Gable who comforted him, drawing on feelings about the loss of his own young wife, Carol Lombard, in a plane crash during the war. Niven remarried in 1948 and remained with his second wife until his death on July 29, 1983.

After Great Britain declared war in 1939, David Niven was one of the first actors to rejoin the army. Despite the fact that he served in the armed forces, he managed to play in two films during that time, both for the war effort. These were *The First of the Few* (1942) and *The Way Ahead* (1944).

After the war, he returned to Hollywood, and was made *Legionnaire of The Order of Merit*, the highest American order that can ever be earned by a foreigner. General Dwight D. Eisenhower presented it to him.

David Niven appeared in over 90 films during his prolific career.

Source: https://www.imdb.com/name/nm0000057/bio
Photo by Silver Screen Collection / Getty Images

Dorothy Dandridge: A Tragic Life (1922-1965)

Dorothy Jean Dandridge was born in Cleveland Ohio's City Hospital on November 9, 1922. Her mother, Ruby Dandridge, was an aspiring actress who had another daughter named Vivian. She walked out on her husband, Cyrus, determined to make it on her own. She took on the task of raising her two girls by herself, moving into an apartment and doing whatever work she could find. She usually cleaned houses, but also sang and recited poetry for local theater groups and churches. A friend named Geneva soon moved in with them, and this new woman was instrumental in teaching the Dandridge girls singing, dancing and the piano. Geneva was also their mother's lover.

The Dandridge sisters, under the tutelege of Ruby and Geneva, became *The Wonder Children* and the foursome-moved to Nashville where they were signed with the National Baptist Convention to tour churches throughout the southern states. Their act was a family affair, with Geneva at the piano, Dorothy and Vivian singing, dancing and reciting and Mama Ruby mostly behind the scenes handling the business affairs of the group. They spent three years on the road but had little time for fun. Education also took a back seat, although both girls were tutored.

Soon friend, Etta Jones, joined the group, and they became a singing trio known as "The Dandridge Sisters." They landed their first big break in the film, *The Big Broadcast,* in 1936.

In 1937, they got a bit part in the Marx Brothers comedy, *A Day At the Races*. In the summer of 1938, the girls were booked at the prestigious *Cotton Club* in New York City. In 1940, Dorothy branched out on her own, and was teamed with the Nicholas Brothers in *Chattanooga Choo Choo*. On September 6, 1942, she and Harold Nicholas were married.

They had one child, a daughter named Harolyn, who was born with disabilities in 1943. Dorothy was unhappy with her husband, who was known for his roving eye, and the marriage broke up in 1949. She was devastated by her daughter's malady, which was diagnosed as mental retardation.

Dorothy had a very successful nightclub act, which in May of 1951 led to numerous television appearances. She was the first black woman to perform at the Waldorf Astoria in New York. In 1954, she landed the part that made her a star in Otto Preminger's *Carmen Jones*. For her work in this film, she was the first African-American actress to be Oscar-nominated for *Best Actress In A Leading Role*. This film also marked the beginning of a long and troubled affair with Preminger himself.

In June of 1959, Dorothy married white restaurant owner, Jack Denison, who by all accounts, was a gold digger after her money. He abused her and about this time she began to drink heavily.

She died on September 8, 1965, from an overdose of barbiturates, which may or may not have been accidental. She was only 43 years old.

Source: https://www.imdb.com/name/nm0199268/bio
Photo: Getty Images

Elizabeth Taylor: An Ageless Beauty (1932- 2011)

Elizabeth Rosemond Taylor entered the world on February 27, 1932 in London, England. She was born a British subject, but her parents were American art dealers from St Louis. Her mother had been an actress on the stage before her marriage to Elizabeth's father and Elizabeth lived in London until 1939 when she was seven years old. At that time, the family returned to America, settling in Los Angeles.

A family friend suggested that the strikingly beautiful little Elizabeth be taken for a screen test and when she did, Universal Pictures immediately signed her to a contract. She debuted in the film, *There's One Born Every Minute* in 1942, which was released when she was ten years of age. Universal dropped her contract after the film, but MGM picked it up, and she signed on for three more films, *Lassie Come Home* (1943, *Jane Eyre* (1944) and *The White Cliffs of Dover* (1944).

The picture that made her famous was *National Velvet* (1944) in which she played Velvet Brown opposite Mickey Rooney. The film was a smash hit and grossed over $4 million. She was MGM's top child star with a long-term contract. Her next film was *The Courage of Lassie*, which she made in 1946. *Life With Father* was produced the following year, in which she appeared with William Powell and Irene Dunne. Her busiest year was 1954 when she made five films, including: *Rhapsody*,

Beau Brummell, The Last Time I Saw Paris and *Elephant Walk.* At that time, she was 22 and considered one of the world's greatest beauties.

She won an Oscar in 1960 for her excellent portrayal of a call girl in *Butterfield 8,* but there were no more films for Liz until she did *Cleopatra* in 1963. She won a second Oscar for her role of Martha in the 1966 film, *Who's Afraid of Virginia Woolf?*

Her private life was rocky with many life-threatening illnesses, including a brain tumor, which was removed in 1997. She had been married eight times, twice to Richard Burton. A great humanitarian, she supported the cause of AIDS long before it was a popular thing to do so.

A beautiful woman to the end, Liz Taylor died of congestive heart failure in 2011.

Source: https://www.imdb.com/name/nm0000072/bio
Photo by Silver Screen Collection / Getty Images

Fatty Arbuckle:
A Scandalous Career
(1887-1933)

Roscoe Conking "Fatty" Arbuckle was born on March 24, 1887 at Smith Center, Kansas. Supposedly, he entered the world weighing in at 16 pounds. He was the youngest of nine children and his family moved to California when he was about a year old. By the age of eight, he was already appearing in stage productions and his first part was with the Webster-Brown Stock Company. He continued to work on stage until 1913, at which point he was hired by Keystone to appear in hundreds of "one reel comedies." Usually he played a cop alongside the *Keystone Cops*, but he also worked with Mabel Normand and Charlie Chaplin.

By 1915, he had moved up to the "two-reelers," which required the sustenance of comedy, at which, he was very successful. He appeared in: *Fatty Again* (1914); *Mabel, Fatty And The Law* (1915); *Mabel and Fatty's Wash Day* (1915); *Mabel And Fatty Viewing The World's Fair At San Francisco* (1915) and others. By 1917, he had formed a partnership company, *Comique*, with Joseph M. Schenk, who was the husband of Norma Talmadge. Arbuckle hired Buster Keaton, whom he had met on the streets of New York, and his career took off with Arbuckle's production of *The Butcher Boy* (1917).

But scandal reared its ugly head on Labor Day, 1921, with the arrest of Arbuckle on manslaughter charges in the death of starlet,

Virginia Rappe, who fell ill and died during a party in his private suite. The Hearst papers made the most of this first Hollywood scandal, and although Arbuckle was eventually acquitted of all charges after a third trial in 1923, his career was finished.

Unable to return to the screen, he worked as a comedy director under the assumed name of William Goodrich. In 1933, he signed a contract with Sam Sax to appear in a short for Warner Brothers.

Although he did six shorts successfully and Warner Brothers signed him to a feature film contract, a new career was not in the cards for the one time star.

He died of a heart attack in his sleep at the age of 46 the night after he signed the contract.

Source: https://en.wikipedia.org/wiki/Roscoe_Arbuckle
Photo by Hulton Archive / Getty Images

**Frank Sinatra:
Old Blue Eyes Never Left!
(1915-1998)**

Born on December 12, 1915, in Hoboken, New Jersey, Francis Albert Sinatra was the only child of a quiet Sicilian-born fireman and a tempestuous Ligurian mother (Natalia Della aka Dolly). His childhood was actually conventionally middle class due to the stability of his father's job as a fireman. He decided he wanted to become a singer very early in life, after hearing Bing Crosby croon on the radio. And sing he did, in many small clubs in New Jersey until one lucky night he attracted the attention of trumpeter and bandleader, Harry James.

After a brief stint with James, Sinatra joined the Tommy Dorsey Orchestra in 1940 where he rose to fame as a singer. While he was a featured performer with the Dorsey band, he made his early film appearances in little known musicals like *Ship Ahoy* with Eleanor Powell in 1942. His singing career was in decline in the late 1940s and early 1950s, but Sinatra made an astonishing comeback as a serious actor in 1953 with his fine performance as Pvt. Angelo Maggio in *From Here To Eternity*, for which he won a Best Supporting Actor Academy Award.

The following few years cast him in important roles such as a psychopathic killer in *Suddenly* in 1954 and as a heroin addict in *The Man With the Golden Arm* (1955), for which he received an Academy Award Best Actor nomination.

He also revived his singing career during the 1950s, signing with Capitol records and working with some of the finest musical arrangers of the era, notably Nelson Riddle, Gordon Jenkins and Billy May. By the early 1960s, he started his own recording label, Reprise Records, and his position with that label earned him the nickname, *The Chairman of The Board*.

He became a popular attraction in Las Vegas along with his pals, Dean Martin, Peter Lawford, Joey Bishop and Sammy Davis, Jr, who were known collectively as the *Rat Pack*. He played a major role in the desegregation of Nevada hotels and casinos in the 1960s.

He had a full successful life, dying of a heart attack on May 14, 1998, at the age of 82.

He had married three times and had three children: Nancy, Frank Sinatra, Jr. (deceased) and Christine.

Source: https://www.biography.com/people/frank-sinatra-9484810
Photo by Gjon Mili / The LIFE Picture Collection / Getty Images

**Fred Astaire:
The Dancing King
(1899-1987)**

On May 10, 1899, in Omaha, Nebraska, Frederick Austerlitz came into the world eighteen months after his sister, Adele.

The son of an Austrian immigrant and traveling salesman, four-year-old Fred used to accompany his older sister to ballet school where she exhibited an early talent for dancing. In 1904, Mama Austerlitz, wanting only the best for her children, moved to New York and enrolled them in a performing arts school run by Ned Wayburn, who was considered one of the pioneers of modern tap dancing. The brother and sister team debuted in New Jersey and began touring on the popular Orpheum Circuit. Most of Fred's early schooling was done under his mother's tutelage while he was on the road.

They changed their name to Astaire at the time of World War One, when anti-German sentiment was very prevalent. In 1917, he and his sister, Adele, made their Broadway debut in the musical revue, *Over The Top*. It wasn't until 1922, however, when they first began to get noticed by the powers-that-Broadway-be. Their big break came when they were both cast in *For Goodness Sake*, a musical, which featured songs written by George and Ira Gershwin.

Throughout the 1920s, the brother and sister team flourished and performed in such hits as *Funny Face* and *Lady Be Good*. Sister Adele retired in 1932, leaving brother Fred to fend for himself.

Fred made his film debut in 1933 in *Dancing Lady*. His role as an accordion player in the movie, *Flying Down To Rio* in 1933 matched him up with the lovely Ginger Rogers for the first time and the rest is more or less celluloid history.

Ironically, Fred Astaire, who was always depicted in formal wear as he "put on the Ritz," hated to get dressed up and considered a tux and tails his work clothes.

He died in 1987 at the age of 88.

Source: https://www.biography.com/people/fred-astaire-9190991
Photo by NBC/NBCU Photo Bank via Getty Images

Gary Cooper:
A True Leading Man
(1901-1961)

Frank James Cooper was born on
May 7, 1901, in Helena, Montana,
but as a child lived in the land of
his heritage, Dunstable, England.

He and his older brother, Arthur Le
Roy, attended grammar school in
Dunstable between 1910 and 1913.
At the age of thirteen, he was
injured in an automobile accident
and moved to his father's cattle ranch in Montana to recuperate.
There he learned to ride horses and became friendly with his
neighbor, ten year old Myrna Loy.

He moved to Los Angeles as a young man in 1924 where he hoped
to pursue a career as an artist in the advertising industry. After a
few months, he discovered he was not suitable for the advertising
world, and drifted into the burgeoning motion picture industry.

He worked as an extra for almost a year before landing a real
part in a "two reeler" opposite Eileen Sedgewick. Paramount
soon offered him a contract and he changed his first name to
Gary on the advice of his agent.

Gary Cooper appeared in more than one hundred films over the
course of his almost three decade career. Known as "Coop" to
his friends and colleagues, he won his first Academy Award for
Best Actor in 1941 for his work in the film, *Sergeant York*.

His second Academy Award came in 1952 for his much-acclaimed performance as Marshall Will Kane opposite Grace Kelly in *High Noon*.

He had many well-publicized affairs before marrying Veronica Balfe, a Roman Catholic socialite with whom he had one daughter, Maria. Despite his conversion to Catholicism to please his wife and other promises, he had affairs while married as well, both with co-stars, Patricia Neal and Grace Kelly.

He died at the age of 60 from lung cancer on May 13, 1961. He has a star on the Hollywood Walk of Fame at 6243 Hollywood Boulevard. He was also inducted into the Western Performers Hall of Fame in Oklahoma City in 1966. Irving Berlin immortalized his name in his song, *Puttin' On The Ritz*, with the line, *Tryin' hard to look like Gary Cooper (super duper)*.

Source: https://www.imdb.com/name/nm0000011/bio
Photo by Hulton Archive / Getty Images

Gene Kelly:
Dancer Everyman
(1910-1996)

Gene Kelly himself once said of his dancing, "If Fred Astaire is the aristocracy, then I am the proletariat." Born Eugene Curran Kelly on August 23, 1910, in Pittsburgh, Pennsylvania, his father was Al Jolson's road manager in the 1920s. He graduated from the University of Pittsburgh with a degree in economics. During World War II, he was a sailor and starred in several films made for the Navy. While on leave, he also did some civilian films.

A dancer since childhood, Gene graduated from college during The Great Depression when jobs were scarce. He was forced to take menial jobs to support himself. He was once a dancing teacher, and eventually he managed to get a chorus-boy assignment on the Broadway stage.

His rise to stardom was quick and occurred shortly after 1940 when he won the leading role in Rodgers and Hart's production of *Pal Joey*. He arrived in Hollywood in 1941, preparing to return to the Broadway stage after making the one film called for in his contract. But he remained, for he found personal and artistic fulfillment there, even after he finished his first film for MGM opposite Judy Garland, *For Me And My Gal*.

Surely his best known dancing steps can be seen by all the world in the musical bulls-eye, *Singin' In The Rain*, all of which he choreographed himself. With co-stars Donald O'Connor and Debbie Reynolds, the gala musical about Hollywood's switch from silent to talking films was a smash hit. The plot may have been silly and weak in parts, but the golden feet of Kelly and his co-stars shine a wonderful light all the way through the film.

Gene Kelly was married twice and had three children, two girls and a boy. His two wives, Betsy Blair and Jeanne Coyne, were both dancers.

He made more than forty films and his career spanned four decades. He died on February 6, 1996.

Source: https://www.imdb.com/name/nm0000037/bio
Photo by Alfred Eisenstaedt / Time & Life Pictures / Getty Images

Gene Tierney: She Walks In Beauty (1920-1991)

Gene Eliza Tierney was born in Brooklyn, New York on November 19, 1920. Her parents were well-to-do; her father a successful insurance broker and her mother a former school teacher. Her lavish childhood was spent in New York and also at times in Connecticut with her wealthy grandparents. She was educated at the finest schools on the East Coast and went to finishing school in Switzerland. After two years in Europe, she returned to America where she completed her education.

By 1939, she was performing on Broadway and her indulgent and wealthy father helped her career by setting up a corporation the purpose of which was to promote her theatrical pursuits. In her first appearance, she is seen carrying a water bucket across the stage. One critic said, "Miss Tierney is, without a doubt, the most beautiful water-carrier I have ever seen!"

But Gene was an actress of substance as well as a beauty, and soon Darryl F. Zanuck spotted her and signed her to a contract with 20th-Century-Fox. Her first movie role was in *Hudson's Bay* in 1941. During that same year, she appeared in *The Return of Jesse James* and within a few years, after several masterful performances under her belt, she was nominated for a *Best Actress Oscar* for her portrayal of Ellen Brent in *Leave Her To Heaven*.

Perhaps her best known role is as Laura Hunt in Otto Preminger's masterful thriller, *Laura*.

Gene Tierney suffered from depression and received many shock treatments in the 1950s. The pressures of a failed marriage to designer, Oleg Cassini, the birth of a mentally retarded daughter in 1943 and several unhappy love affairs resulted in her downward spiral and hospitalization.

She had an affair with John F. Kennedy, whom she met while filming *Dragonwyck* in 1946. Kennedy broke it off because of his political aspirations, but Gene also had affairs with Tyrone Power and Prince Aly Khan.

True happiness eluded this beautiful film legend, who died on November 6, 1991, just two weeks shy of her 71st birthday.

Source:
https://www.bestmoviesbyfarr.com/articles/gene-tierney-pictures/2015/11
Photo: Creator: Donaldson Collection Credit: Getty Images

George Sanders: The Classic Cad (1906-1972)

He was born to English parents in St. Petersburg, Russia, on July 3, 1906. George Sanders and his family returned to England when the Russian Revolution began. He entered the world of acting when a secretary named Greer Garson, who was working in the same advertising firm, suggested the idea to him. Previously, he had worked in the tobacco business, a Birmingham textile mill and as an advertising writer. He started in show business on the bottom rung of the ladder, as a chorus boy.

He worked his way up diligently through cabaret, radio and as a theatrical understudy. His British film debut was in 1936 when he appeared as Curly Randall in *Find The Lady*. He appeared in the United States for the first time the following year in Twentieth Century Fox's production of *Lloyd's of London* in which he played Lord Everett Stacy opposite Tyrone Power.

During the late 1930s and early 1940s Sanders branched out in many creative directions, portraying everything from Nazis to undercover agents, royalty and biblical figures. He established a "star" niche for himself as Simon Templar, *The Saint,* and as Gay Lawrence, *The Falcon*. He appeared with his brother, Tom Conway, in *The Falcon's Brother* in 1942. They portrayed brothers in an odd twist of art imitating life. But Sanders grew tired

of the role, and gave it to his brother who took it up for
nine subsequent films through 1946.

He was equally adept in the role of a debonair leading man and
a ruthless cad, but the latter won him more acclaim. His most
famous role and the one that he was born to play, was as a cynical
Broadway critic, Addison De Witt, in *All About Eve* (1950). His
performance earned him an Academy Award for Best Supporting
Actor. In 1940, he appeared in two Hitchcock films, *Rebecca* and
Foreign Correspondent.

George Sanders was a man of many talents. He possessed a
fine baritone singing voice and was a gifted writer as well. His
autobiography, *Memoirs of a Professional Cad,* reveals his sharp
but troubled mind. He was married four times, (once to Zsa Zsa
Gabor and once to her sister, Magda) but was happiest with Benita
Hume who died 8 years after their union.

He committed suicide in Barcelona, Spain, on April 25, 1972.
He left a note that read in part, "Dear World, I am leaving because
I am bored."

He left a film legacy of many fine performances in a career that
spanned almost four decades.

Source: https://www.imdb.com/name/nm0001695/bio
Photo Source: Photo by Pictorial Parade / Archive Photos / Getty Images

**Gloria Swanson:
Grande Dame
of The Silent Era
(1899-1983)**

Born March 27, 1899 in
Chicago, Illinois, Gloria May
Josephine Svenson was one
of the biggest stars of the
silent movie era.

As a child, she attended public
schools in Chicago, Key West, Florida and San Juan, Puerto Rico.
She made her film debut
in 1915 as an extra in the film, *The Fable of Elvira and Farina*
and *The Meal Ticket.* Soon she had leading roles in pictures
with many different directors, landing a contract with Cecil B.
DeMille in 1919.

It was De Mille who transformed Gloria from a typical
comedienne-type actress into a vibrant star. Gloria collected
husbands and lovers like some people collect bone china.
Joseph Kennedy (father of the slain president) produced her
Queen Kelly in 1929, which was directed by Erich Von Stroheim
and was the film that her character, Norma Desmond, was
watching in *Sunset Boulevard.*

Many actors and actresses did not survive the switch from silent
film to talkies, but Gloria Swanson did. In *Music in the Air* (1934)
she re-invented herself enough to even learn how to sing. Still, her
kind of movies weren't being made any longer and she remained a
throwback from another time and place. She did return to the stage

in the 1940s and appeared in *Reflected Glory*, *Let's Be Gay* and *A Goose For The Gander*.

She received Best Actress nominations for *Sadie Thompson* (1928), *The Trespasser* (1929), and *Sunset Boulevard* (1950).

She became a clothes designer and founded a line of cosmetics (*Essence of Nature*). She also made many cameo television appearances throughout the 1960s and 1970s and promoted health foods. Her last film was *Airport 75* in which she played herself.

Gloria was married five times and had two children. She died on April 4, 1983, at the age of 84.

Source: https://www.imdb.com/name/nm0841797/bio
Photo by Hulton Archive / Getty Images

Grace Kelly:
Lovely Princess Of Monaco
(1929-1982)

Grace Patricia Kelly was born
in Philadelphia, Pennsylvania,
to wealthy parents on November
12, 1929.

Her father was from a prominent
Irish family; her mother, Katherine
Majer, was a German convert
from Lutheranism. Grace knew
she wanted to become an actress
at a very early age, and after graduating from high school in 1947,
she traveled to New York
in search of bright lights and success.

Her family was opposed to her becoming an actress, and she
found work first as a fashion model. In 1949, she made her
Broadway debut and she also appeared on television. She soon
moved to California, however, drawn to the promise of work
in motion pictures.

At the age of twenty-two in 1951, Grace nabbed her first film role
in *Fourteen Hours*. The following year marked her big break as
Amy Kane in *High Noon* opposite Gary Cooper, with whom she
had an affair. In 1953, she appeared in *Mogambo* opposite Ava
Gardner and Clark Gable, with whom she also had an affair.

Grace would not become a star, however, until 1954 when Alfred
Hitchcock cast her in his classic thriller, *Dial M For Murder*
opposite Ray Milland, who fell in love with her. Grace then made

Rear Window later that same year, and won an Academy Award for Best Actress in *The Country Girl (also 1954)*. Her last Hitchcock film was *To Catch A Thief* in 1955, on the set of which she met her husband-to-be, Prince Ranier of Monaco.

Grace Kelly appeared in eleven films, her last performance in *High Society* (1956) with Frank Sinatra and Bing Crosby. On April 19, 1956, she became *Her Serene Highness Princess Grace of Monaco*, and she gave up her acting career. She had three children with Ranier, two girls and one boy.

On September 14, 1982, her life ended tragically in an automobile accident along the rocky, twisty and mountainous roads of Monaco. She was only fifty-two years old.

She is the first actress ever to have her face appear on a postage stamp.

Source: https://www.biography.com/people/grace-kelly-9362226
Photo: PA Images Credit: PA Images via Getty Images.

Gregory Hines:
A Man of Many Talents
(1946-2003)

Gregory Oliver Hines entered the world on February 14, 1946. Unfortunately, he left it too soon, dying of liver cancer at the age of 57 on August 9, 2003. In between was a life of accolades, artistic expression and rewards for his outstanding talent. An accomplished tap dancer and choreographer, Gregory Hines is credited with having kept the art of big screen tap dancing alive. He also made many films and was a capable actor.

He entered show business at the tender age of six with his brother, Maurice, appearing at the Apollo Theater in Harlem as *The Hines Kids*. Later, he was part of a tap-dancing trio act that featured both his brother, Maurice, and dad. *Hines, Hines and Dad* was the beginning of the development of a "show biz savvy" that would follow him for all of his formidable life.

His film debut was in 1981 when he played a Roman slave in Mel Brook's hilarious film, *History of The World: Part 1*. Three years later he was a thinly disguised Nicholas Brother in *The Cotton Club* in 1984. His own brother appeared in this film, and in true art imitating life fashion, played his brother in the film! In an ironic twist, the movie was set in the same Harlem nightclub where Hines's own grandmother had been an entertainer performing for a white audience back in the 1920s and 30s. In 1985, he danced opposite ballet star, Mikhail Baryshnikov, in the film, *White Nights*.

He was married twice and left two children. His accomplishments are too numerous to mention here in full detail. He won many awards for his talents, including a Tony for the Broadway musical, *Jelly's Last Jam*, in 1992.

The world not only lost a fine performer but also a fine human being on the day this talented, sleepy-eyed, silky-smooth entertainer took his last breath.

Source: https://www.biography.com/people/gregory-hines-9542572
Photo: Jack Mitchell / Getty Images.

Gregory Peck:
A Classic
Man Among Men
(1911-2003)

Born Eldred Gregory Peck in 1916, this handsome star of stage and screen began his life in La Jolla, California. His parents divorced when he was only five, and he went to live with his grandmother of whom he had many fond memories. One of his earliest movie memories concerned being so scared by *The Phantom of The Opera*, which he saw when he was nine, that his grandmother allowed him to sleep in bed with her that night.

He studied pre-med at Berkeley, but the acting bug bit him shortly after graduation. He moved to New York and enrolled at the Neighborhood Playhouse. He debuted on Broadway in 1942 in *The Morning Star*. After a year or so on stage, he returned to California to appear in another film, *Days of Glory*. But it was his next role in 1944 as a Roman Catholic priest in *Keys of The Kingdom* that soared him to stardom, and earned him his first Academy Award nomination.

His paternal grandmother, Catherine Ashe, was an immigrant from Ireland and she was related to Thomas Ashe, an Irish patriot who died in 1917. His paternal grandfather had Armenian roots and emigrated from England. Gregory Peck actually took classes in the Armenian language in his middle age to bring him closer to his Armenian roots.

Of all the many movies he made, *To Kill A Mockingbird* was his personal favorite. About this role he said, "I put everything I had into it; all my feelings and everything I'd learned in 46 years of living, about family life and fathers and children. And my feelings about racial justice and inequality and opportunity."

He had five children, one of whom, Jonathan, was his spitting image. Jonathan took his own life by gunshot in 1975. Peck almost always played courageous men who saw injustice and fought it.

He died in June 2003, survived by his wife and four children, and Brock Peters, his co-star in *To Kill a Mockingbird*, performed the eulogy.

Source: https://www.imdb.com/name/nm0000060/bio
Photo: Reporters Associes Credit: Gamma-Rapho via Getty Images

Humphrey Bogart: An Actor With a Following (1899-1957)

Born Humphrey De Forest Bogart in New York City on December 25, 1899, this unlikely star was the son of a prominent Manhattan surgeon, Belmont Bogart, and Maude Humphreys, a well-known magazine illustrator. He was of Dutch, English and Spanish heritage and distantly related to the late Princes Diana, through her American relations. His mother often used him as a model for her many illustrations of children, and when he was a baby, he appeared in a national advertising campaign for Mellin's baby food.

He was educated at the Trinity School in New York City and then sent to Phillips Academy in Andover, Massachusetts in preparation for medical studies at Yale. He was expelled from Phillips and joined the Naval Reserve instead, much to the chagrin of his parents.

Between 1920-1922, he managed a stage company that was owned by a family friend, William A Brady. He performed on stage until 1930 when he earned a contract with Fox and a debut in a ten-minute short called: *Broadway's Like That*, which co-starred Ruth Etting and Joan Blondell.

It took another five years of working on stage and in minor film roles before he finally got his big break in 1936 with the role of

Duke Mantee in *The Petrified Forest,* which starred Betty Davis and Leslie Howard. He got the part largely through the influence of his friend, Leslie Howard, with whom he had appeared in the Broadway production of the film. Bogart named one of his children Leslie, to show his gratitude to his friend.

He was known as the tough, savvy and occasionally reckless character who lived in a world of corruption but nurtured his own hidden moral agenda. Ironically, almost all of the films that made him a star, such as *High Sierra* in 1941, *The Maltese Falcon* and *Casablanca* in 1942, were roles that were originally offered to and rejected by George Raft. In an even greater twist of fate, Bogart became a far better known star, and is considered by most critics to be the superior actor of the two.

Although he had married four times, he found true happiness with his fourth and final wife, Lauren Bacall, who was thirty years his junior. He even joked that the "something old" of the "something old, something new, something borrowed and something blue" wedding ditty referred to the groom.

Upon his death from throat cancer on January 14, 1957, his wife placed a golden whistle in his coffin.

He left a lasting legacy of remarkable films.

Source: https://www.biography.com/people/humphrey-bogart-9217486
Photo: Silver Screen Collection / Getty Images

Jack Lemmon: Versatility Personified (1925-2001)

There are few actors with the range of talent and versatility exhibited by this fine star of stage and screen.

Born Jack Uhler Lemmon III in an elevator in Newton, Massachusetts, on February 8, 1925, his father was a successful businessman (president of a doughnut company).

He described his flamboyant and authoritarian mother, as "Tallulah Bankhead on a road show." As a young man, he attended Phillip's Academy and Harvard University where he was the president of The Hasty Pudding Club. He graduated with a degree in "War Service Sciences." During World War II, he served in the Navy, and after the war he embarked on an acting career on radio and on Broadway.

His father did not approve of his son's choice of careers, but told him to pursue his dream as long as he felt a passion for it. Jack followed his father's advice, and his dying words of "spread a little sunshine." He went unnoticed in his very first bit part, which he landed in the 1949 film, T*he Lady Takes A Sailor.* It wouldn't be until 1954 when he appeared opposite Judy Holiday in the film, *It Should Happen To You,* that his great talent was appreciated and rewarded.

He was very well liked among other actors, including Ving Rhames, who upon winning an Oscar for Best Actor in a television movie in 1998, gave his award to Jack Lemmon to express his admiration for his expertise and talent.

Although he made many wonderful films before dying of cancer in June of 2001, Jack Lemmon is perhaps best remembered for the fact that he did drama as well as he did comedy.

This fact is no more aptly illustrated than his outstanding performances in; *The Odd Couple* with co-star and friend, Walter Matthau; *Some Like It Hot* opposite Marilyn Monroe and Tony Curtis and his powerful portrayal as an alcoholic in *The Days of Wine And Roses* with Lee Remick.

Source: https://www.biography.com/people/jack-lemmon-9378762
Photo: Ann Clifford Credit: The LIFE Picture Collection / Getty Images

James Stewart:
A Man Among Stars
(1909-1997)

James Maitland Stewart was born to Scots-Irish parents in Indiana, Pennsylvania, on May 20, 1909. His father ran a hardware store, and when he won the Academy Award for best actor in 1941 in *The Philadelphia Story*, the Oscar was kept in the window of the store ironically located on Philadelphia Street in Indiana, Pennsylvania. Even though "Philadelphia" was misspelled, the trophy remained in the store window for twenty-five years.

This brilliant star of stage and screen never took an acting lesson in his life. He personally felt that people could learn more when actually working than studying the craft. Highly educated, he graduated in 1932 from Princeton University with a degree in architecture. But the acting bug bit after graduation when fellow classmate, Josh Logan, convinced him to join the newly formed University Players. Some of the other members included Margaret Sullivan and Henry Fonda, with whom he would maintain a life-long friendship. He went to Hollywood in 1935 as the ideal incarnation of the American Everyman.

James Stewart was the first Hollywood star to enter the armed services for World War II. He joined in 1940, the year before Pearl Harbor. Although he was five pounds less than the required minimum weight of 148 pounds, he talked the recruitment officer into admitting him. He eventually became a Colonel and earned *The Air Medal, The Distinguished Flying Cross, The Croix de Guerre* and seven *Battle Stars*. In 1959, serving in the Air Force Reserve, James Stewart became a Brigadier General, making him the highest-ranking entertainer in the US Military.

In 1949 he married Gloria Hatrick McLean, who had two children from a previous marriage (one of whom would die in Vietnam). He and Gloria had twin daughters, Judy and Kelly. By all accounts, he remained faithful to his wife, which was unusual for a Hollywood leading man.

In the 1950s, he negotiated for a percentage of the profits of his films and became wealthy. He remained active in his career throughout the seventies and even through the 80s and early 90s. He is a cultural icon and his persona lives in the patriotic spirit embodied in all of us. He died in 1997 of a thrombosis that formed in his right leg, which led to a pulmonary embolism a week later. His wife, who died a few years before, was the subject of his last words to his family which were: "I'm going to be with Gloria now."

Of all the movies he ever made, his role as George Bailey in *It's a Wonderful Life*, which was made in 1946 and directed by Frank Capra, was his personal favorite.

Source: https://www.imdb.com/name/nm0000071/bio
Photo: Hulton Archive Credit: Getty Images

Jeff Chandler:
Tall Dark And Handsome
(1918-1961)

Born Ira Grossel in Brooklyn, New York, on December 15, 1918, this future star of stage and screen stood six feet four inches tall at fifteen years of age! He began to gray at the temples when he was only eighteen, perhaps a poetic omen of the fact that he would not live to be old. He graduated Erasmus Hall High School, and was a childhood friend and neighbor of Susan Hayward.

After high school, he took a drama course, and for the next two years, worked in various stock companies. He kept his real name all through World War II where he served as an officer, and during a successful radio career, in which he co-starred with Eve Arden in *Our Miss Brooks*.

When he signed up with Universal Studios, he changed his name to Jeff Chandler. His first appearance in film was as a supporting player in *Johnny O'Clock* (1947). He played in many different types of films, including westerns, dramas, action films and "soapers." He appeared opposite the best and most beautiful; Rhonda Fleming, Lana Turner, Ann Baxter and Maureen O'Hara, just to name a few. In 1950 he was nominated for an Academy Award for his role as Cochise in the film, *Broken Arrow*.

Jeff Chandler also enjoyed success as a recording artist. He wrote music, played the violin, owned the Chandler Music Company and recorded several successful albums for Liberty Records. He injured his back while on the set of what would be his last film, *Merrill's Marauders*.

His death on June 17, 1961 at the age of 43 following surgery for a herniated disc was deemed malpractice. It resulted in a large lawsuit and settlement for his daughters, Jamie and Dana.

His kindness was not publicized, but it was there. In a gesture of pure friendship, when Sammy Davis Jr. lost an eye in an accident and was in danger of losing the other, Jeff Chandler offered to give Davis one of his own eyes.

He left a legacy of more than forty films.

Source: https://en.wikipedia.org/wiki/Jeff_Chandler
Photo: Michael Ochs Archives Credit: Getty Images

Jimmy Cagney: Great American, Great Actor (1899-1986)

What was it about Jimmy Cagney that made him so beloved by so many fans? Read on for a bit about his magic and charm.

Born in The Yorkville section of Manhattan, New York, on July 19, 1899, to Irish and Norwegian parents, James Cagney entered show business shortly after World War One. He auditioned for a group of vaudevillians who were seeking dancers and singers, and while he could do neither, he somehow managed to land the job for $35 dollars a week. The red-haired, blue-eyed, five-eight, 180 pound Cagney graduated from Stuyvesant High School and attended Columbia University.

The world of Vaudeville was his home until 1929 when he left for Broadway to star with Joan Blondell in *Penny Arcade*. A subsequent offer to go to Hollywood for a screen test landed him a part in the 1930 film, *Sinners Holiday*. He became typecast as a mean little gangster even though his talents far exceeded the roles assigned to him. He begged the studio to give him other parts, claiming that he was "tired of beating up on women," but his success in these roles, in *Public Enemy* (1931, *The Roaring Twenties (1939)* and While Heat (1949) mired him in cinematic place, at least for a while.

In 1942, Cagney found the role that would change the course of his career forever. *Yankee Doodle Dandy*, which was the life story

of colorful showman, George M. Cohan, featured his wonderful
dancing. His performance earned him an Academy Award. Cohan
himself approved of Cagney as the portrayer of his very significant
life shortly before his own death in November of that same year.

Cagney retired from the cinema in 1961 and moved to his
800-acre ranch in Duchess County, New York, with his wife,
Frances ("Bill") Willard Cagney, whom he had married in 1921.

He returned to the movies only once in 1980 to make the film,
Ragtime, with his old friend, Pat O'Brien.

The master of improvisation died on March 30, 1986, leaving
a legacy of more than seventy films and millions of adoring
fans all over the world.

Source: https://www.imdb.com/name/nm0000010/bio
Photo by Silver Screen Collection / Getty Images

Joan Crawford:
A Star Tormented
(1904-1977)

Born Lucille Fay Le Sueur, Joan Crawford entered the world on March 3, 1904 in San Antonio, Texas. Her parents had separated before she was born, and her mother married three times. By age sixteen, Lucille had known three fathers, one of whom was a vaudeville theater manager who named her Billie Cassin. The year 1915 found her living with her mother in Kansas City where "Billie" worked in a laundry in order to pay for her school tuition. Despite her dismal surroundings, Lucille made her own fun. She was fond of and entered many dance contests. One such contest led to chorus work in Chicago, Detroit and New York in 1923.

She left for Hollywood on New Years Day, 1925. A Photoplay contest led to the adoption of the name, Joan Crawford, and in 1928, with her performance *in Our Dancing Daughters*, she became a star. She had a string of successes with MGM and after 18 years, in 1943 left to sign with another studio, Warner Brothers.

She won her first Oscar for her work in *Mildred Pierce* (1945). Specializing in suffering, her roles always dictated that she wear pearls and hold her head high. She often took parts in which she was a woman of lower class origins who struggled to succeed (usually on the back of a wealthy man) in the big, mean old city.

She married Alfred Steele, Chairman of the Board of Pepsi Cola, after making more than seventy films. She remained with the company after his death in 1959 until 1972 when the-powers-that-be pushed her out. *Whatever Happened to Baby Jane?* renewed her career as a cinema star in 1962, but she and Bette Davis hated each other and never worked together again.

She retired from the public eye in 1974 and devoted herself to Christian Science and vodka. In her New York City brownstone, she was a recluse who died on May 10, 1977. Her four adopted children received little money from her two million dollar estate and two of them, Christopher and Christina, received nothing "for", as she so enigmatically wrote in her will, "reasons known best to them."

Source: https://en.wikipedia.org/wiki/Joan_Crawford
Photo by Bert Six / John Kobal Foundation / Getty Images

Joseph Cotton:
A First Rate Third Man
(1905-1994)

Joseph Cheshire Cotton was born in Petersburg, Virginia, on May 15, 1905. He had a career as an advertiser and as a theater critic before becoming an actor.

It was his friendship with veteran actor, Orson Welles, that gave him his start as an actor at both The Federal Theater (1936) and with his group, The Mercury Players (1937). In 1941, Cotton followed Welles to Hollywood and made his film debut in Welles' classic film based on the life of William Randolph Hearst, *Citizen Kane*. As Jed Leland, he portrayed the Great Man's friend and a drama critic (both roles which he also played in real life).

After appearing in another film, *Lydia,* that same year, Cotton once again teamed up with his friend, Welles, for two more films in 1942, *The Magnificent Ambersons* and *Journey Into Fear*. These films were not great successes for Welles, but they proved sufficient vehicles for Cotton's rise to stardom as a leading man. He went on to work with Alfred Hitchcock in the classic mystery, *Shadow of A Doubt* in 1943, and in that same year, *Hers To Hold* opposite Deanna Durbin. *Gaslight* with Ingrid Bergman and Charles Boyer followed in 1944 as well as *Since You Went Away*, *Portrait of Jennie*, *Love Letters* and *Duel in The Sun*.

He played opposite the top female stars of the day, including Jennifer Jones, Bette Davis, Loretta Young and Barbara Stanwyck. He appeared again with Orson Welles in 1949 in the marvelous thriller based on Carol Reed's novel, *The Third Man*. In this film, he plays an American writer caught up in the black market operations of post-war Vienna.

He married the lovely Patricia Medina in 1960, after his first wife, Lenore Kipp La Mont, a pianist and divorcée with one young daughter, died of of Leukemia that same year.

He retired from acting in the 1980s after a stroke and laryngectomy and died on February 6, 1994, at the age of 88.

Source: https://www.imdb.com/name/nm0001072/bio
Photo: Creator: John Kobal Foundation Photo Credit: Getty Images

Josephine Baker: Black Venus Shining (1906-1975)

Born in St. Louis, Missouri, on June 3, 1906, Freda Josephine McDonald was the daughter of Eddie Carson and Carrie McDonald. She left school early to pursue a career on the stage. By age 13, she was performing professionally in vaudeville, making her way towards New York City and the Plantation Club in particular during the Harlem Renaissance. She performed on Broadway in 1922 in the production, *Shuffle Along,* and was already a star by 1924 when she appeared in *Chocolate Dandies.*

The limitations of prejudice imposed upon this blossoming, talented beauty were too much for her, and in 1925 in a daring move, she went to Paris. Here she became famous. On October 2, 1925, she opened at the *Théâter des Champs-Elysées* in the popular *Revue, Negre.* Her dancing was bold and erotic, and she often appeared on stage scantily clad. Still, her dancing always had a graceful, magical and tasteful quality about it. Even critics who didn't like the show thought highly of her abilities.

In 1926-1927, she performed at the *Folies Bergère*, setting the standard for her future acts. Perhaps her most famous act was one in which she appeared in a skirt made only of bananas accompanied by her pet leopard, Chiquita. The leopard with her diamond-studded collar often escaped into the orchestra pit, terrorizing musicians.

Because she found more acceptance in France as a "colored" performer than she had in the Unites States, Josephine remained in Paris. She was also a singer of considerable merit, and in July of 1930, she recorded six songs for Columbia Records. Her sensual beauty inspired artwork by Alexander Calder, and George Roualt. Writers such as Hemingway and E.E. Cummings found her work inspiring.

Josephine Baker was also a very brave and patriotic lady. She served with The Red Cross during World War II and, with the fall of France in 1940, became active in the Resistance Movement. She was so well known that even the Nazis were hesitant to touch her. One incredible story from this period concerns the monster, Herman Göring, who invited her to dinner at his chalet one evening. He suspected that she was active in the Resistance Movement and served her some wine that she somehow sensed was poisonous. She managed to excuse herself and escaped to freedom via a laundry chute! Her efforts awarded her *The Croix de Guerre* and a *Medal of The Resistance* in 1946.

Josephine Baker married four times and adopted twelve children, all of different ethnic backgrounds and races, whom she always referred to as her "rainbow tribe." One of her sons, Jean Claude, owns and operates *Chez Josephine* on the West Side of Manhattan, a restaurant devoted to the memory of his famous mother. The week before her death on April 12, 1975, she appeared on the stage in a tribute performance, still able to captivate an audience at the age of 69. She died quietly in her sleep of a cerebral hemorrhage.

Source: https://www.biography.com/people/josephine-baker-9195959
Photo by Keystone-France / Gamma-Keystone via Getty Images

**Katherine Hepburn:
The First Lady
of The Cinema
(1907-2003)**

Born on May 12, 1907,
in Hartford, Connecticut,
Katherine Houghton Hepburn
was the daughter of a doctor
and a suffragette. Her mother was
an early advocate for birth
control and worked side by side
with crusader, Margaret Sanger,
in her early campaigns for women's reproductive rights. Kate was
raised to speak and develop her mind to its highest potential, both
of which she most certainly did!

She was a tomboy and very close to her brother, Tom, who, at
the age of 14, accidentally hung himself while practicing a hanging
trick their father had taught him. It was Kate who found him and
she was devastated both by the discovery and his loss. For many
years afterward she used his birthday, November 8, as her own.
Most of her early schooling took place at home. She did, however,
attend Bryn Mawr College, and it was there where the acting bug
bit her and wouldn't let go.

After graduating college, she appeared in small roles in Broadway
plays and elsewhere. It was in the film, *A Warrior's Husband*
in 1932 that Katherine got her first starring role as Antiope, an
Amazon princess. She was then cast in *A Bill of Divorcement*
later that same year opposite John Barrymore. After this film,
RKO signed her to a contract, and she made five between 1932 and
1934. For her performance in the third, *Morning Glory* (1933), she

won her first Academy Award. Her fourth film, *Little Women,* which was also made in 1933, was the most successful picture of its day.

After a few years of ups and downs, she returned to Broadway to star in *The Philadelphia Story (1940),* and her star rose to its pinnacle and never stopped shining.

She made eight films with Spencer Tracy over a 25-year period, and their off-screen romance lasted for just as long, ending with his death in June of 1967.

She died at the age of 96 in June of 2003, leaving a film legacy that spanned more than sixty years.

Source: https://www.notablebiographies.com/He-Ho/Hepburn-Katharine.html
Photo by Clarence Sinclair Bull / John Kobal Foundation / Getty Images

Laird Cregar:
A Poignant Villain
(1913-1944)

On July 28, 1913, Samuel Laird Cregar was born in Philadelphia, Pennsylvania. He was the youngest of six sons born to wealthy cricket player, Edward Mathews Cregar and Elizabeth Smith Cregar. His father was a member of an internationally known team called *The Gentleman of Philadelphia* who toured the world in the late 1890s and early 1900s. Although from a rich family, Laird worked as a bouncer early in his career and sometimes had to sleep in his car before he became an established actor.

He was a formally trained actor and an alumnus of the Pasadena Playhouse. In 1940, he landed a bit part in *Granny, Get Your Gun*. His bulk, heavy-lidded gaze and coldly sinister voice made him an ideal villain for the film noir genre popularized in the 1940s. Standing 6 foot, 3 inches tall, he was a formidable "bad guy," no better evidenced than in his memorable and chilling portrayal of Jack the Ripper in the 1944 film, *The Lodger*. In this film he appeared opposite the beautiful Merle Oberon, George Saunders and Sir Cedric Hardwicke. This atmospheric thriller sends shudders even up the spines of the most sophisticated movie viewers of today.

In total, he appeared in 16 films, including *Hangover Square* opposite Linda Darnell and *I Wake Up Screaming* with Betty Grable and Victor Mature.

Despite his talent and success, he yearned to be a leading man, and he went on crash diets to achieve this goal. In the film, *Hangover Square*, there are scenes where his clothes are both too small and too large for him.

But his crash campaign to lose weight, (he dropped 200 pounds) proved to be more than his system could endure.

He died of a heart attack on December 9, 1944, at the age of thirty.

Source: https://www.imdb.com/name/nm0187284/
Photo: Creator: Film Favorites Credit: Getty Images

Lana Turner:
Glamour And Sex Appeal
(1921-1995)

February 8, 1921, Julia Jean Turner was born in Wallace, Idaho, to John Virgil and Mildred Frances Cowan Turner. Her mother was only 15 when she married her father, who was a Tennessean by birth. He worked as a clerk but was a known gambler, and he was murdered for his winnings when she was just a child.

Film journalist, William R. Wilkerson, discovered her in 1936, when she was 15, at the *Top Hat Café* in Hollywood. He introduced her to Zeppo Marx, who was also a talent agent, and she was soon signed as Lana Turner to MGM.

In her debut *They Won't Forget* (1937), she earned the nickname, "sweater girl." She was a popular pin-up girl in World War II because of the success of her two 1941 films, *Johnny Eager* and *Ziegfeld Girl*. She also made four films with Clark Gable: *Honkey Tonk* (1941); *Somewhere I'll Find You;* (1942); *Homecoming,* (1948) and *Betrayed*, (1954). Their box office successes.were heightened by rumors about a relationship between the two actors.

Her career hit a new high with the release of the film-noir classic, *The Postman Always Rings Twice* (1946) co-starring John Garfield. Her public persona and personal life were sliding like a runaway roller coaster during the 1950s, and she was married eight times to seven different husbands. Scandal reared its ugly head in the late 1950s when her daughter, Cheryl Crane, fatally stabbed her lover, gangster, Johnny Stompanato.

She appeared in some television roles during the 1970s and 1980s, but for the most part lived quietly outside of the public eye for the remainder of her life.

She died at the age of 74 on June 29, 1995 of complications from throat cancer.

Cheryl Crane, her only child and Cheryl's female life partner, whom Lana accepted as a second daughter, inherited her estate.

Source: https://www.biography.com/people/lana-turner-9542242
Photo by Archive Photos / Getty Images

Laurence Olivier:
King Of Actors
(1907-1989)

Laurence Kerr Olivier was born
on May 22, 1907, in Dorking,
Surrey. It was his father, Gerald
Kerr Olivier, an Anglican priest,
who decided that his son "Kim"
as he was called, would become
the actor in the family. Laurence
received his education at St.
Edward's School in Oxford and
at The Central School of Speech
and Drama.

In 1935, Laurence made his stage debut in Noel Coward's *Private
Lives* followed by *Romeo and Juliet*, where he worked opposite
John Gielgud. He became a star after his film debut in 1939 with
his portrayal of tortured Heathcliff in *Wuthering Heights* opposite
Merle Oberon, Geraldine Fitzgerald and David Niven.

Olivier was married three times and had one son, Tarquin, born
in 1936, from his first wife, Jill Esmond. His second wife was his
most famous one, Vivien Leigh, known for her role as Southern
belle, Scarlet O'Hara, in *Gone With The Wind*. For Olivier, his true
passion was his work, and according to those who knew him best,
he often became despondent when he didn't have a job.

By some critics, Laurence Olivier was the greatest actor who
ever lived. Among his many honors are ten Oscar nominations.
He won two honorary Oscars in 1946, and in 1949, won both
Best Actor and *Best Picture* as the producer for *Hamlet* (1948

movie).He became a "life peer" as Baron Olivier of Brighton in the County of Sussex, and in 1981, was admitted into the Order of Merit.

He died from cancer on July 11, 1989 at the age of 82. He is the second actor to have the honor of being interred in the iconic "Corner"in Westminster Abbey" in London.

In an odd twist of fate, Olivier received top billing in a film fifteen years after his death! In 2004, in *Sky Captain and The World of Tomorrow*, computer technology incorporated footage of Olivier as a young man.

Laurence Olivier left an enormous film legacy.

Source: https://www.imdb.com/name/nm0000059/bio
Photo by Slim Aarons / Getty Images

Loretta Young:
Sweet And Lovely
(1913-2000)

Born in Salt Lake City,
Utah, on January 6, 1913,
Gretchen Michaela Young
was the youngest of three
children. Her mother
moved the family to
Hollywood when
Gretchen was three years
old, where she established a
boarding house. Gretchen's
elder sisters, Polly Ann and
Elizabeth Jane, were child
players on screen, and by the time
she was four years of age, Gretchen joined them and began
working as an extra in films. She left to attend convent school, but
returned to the screen at age 14 with a bit part in *Naughty
But Nice* (1927).

Somewhere along this rocky way, Gretchen became known as
Loretta Young and she gave up her "blonde" look and let her
lovely hair revert back to its natural brown color. She moved
up the ladder quickly, as much due to her genuine talent as her
exquisite good looks. The good girl, Loretta, however, was just
a young impressionable human being, and she made scandalous
headlines when in 1930, at seventeen years of age, she eloped with
Grant Withers, who had appeared with her in the Warner Brothers
production, *The Second Floor Mystery*. Grant had been previously
married and was nine years her senior. The marriage was annulled

the following year. Ironically later in 1931, the pair would again co-star in a film called: *Too Young Too Marry*.

In 1947, she won an *Academy Award for Best Actress* for her performance in the romantic comedy, *The Farmer's Daughter*. In 1953, she retired from the world of films and began a second career as hostess of *Letter To Loretta*, a half-hour television drama series, which ran from September 1953 to September 1961. She frequently starred in the episodes she presented as well.

She was once parodied in a *Mad Magazine* cartoon sequence, which depicted her with her elegant gown getting caught in the door in the middle of one of her dazzling entrances. Although most may remember her for these glittering appearances over the show's eight-year run, Loretta Young was a fine actress who appeared in almost 100 films. She won Emmy awards for *Best Actress in a Dramatic Series* in 1954, 1956 and 1958.

One of the biggest Hollywood secrets did not come out until after her death. She and Clark Gable shared a love child, a daughter who no one ever knew about. The daughter came forward after her mother's death to tell the touching story of how her mother went to Europe in the very early stages of her pregnancy and gave birth to the child. She put the baby up for adoption at a convent and then made arrangements to adopt her.

She died of ovarian cancer at the age of 87 on August 12, 2000 in Los Angeles, California,

Source: https://www.biography.com/people/loretta-young-9542113
Photo by Keystone-France / Gamma-Keystone via Getty Images

Louis Armstrong: The Man With The Golden Horn (1901- 1971)

Louis Daniel Armstrong was born in New Orleans, Louisiana, on August 4, 1901. He grew up in a poor single-parent household and worked at menial jobs even as a little boy. At the age of 13, he celebrated the New Year by running out in the street and firing a pistol that belonged to the current man in his mother's life. This action had him sent to the Colored Waifs Home for Boys, and it seemed his lot in life indeed would be an unhappy one.

But in this home for boys, Louis learned the skill that would make him famous and set him above the rest; he learned to play the bugle and the clarinet. The home had a brass band and Louis joined. For a small fee, the group would often play at socials, picnics and funerals. And so began the career of a musical legend.

In 1918, at the age of 18, Louis got a job in the Kid Ory Band in New Orleans. In 1922, he left for Chicago where he played second coronet in the Creole Jazz Band. With this band he made his first recordings, but his Broadway debut would not come until 1929 when he appeared in *Hot Chocolates*. Here, he introduced Fats Waller's *Ain't Misbehaviing'* which became his very first hit.

In 1932, he toured Europe and performed for the English royalty. During a performance for King George V, he forgot that he had been told that performers were not to refer to members of the royal family while playing for them. Just before beginning a special number, he accidentally said, "This one's for you, Rex."

After this European tour, the gifted musician known by insiders as "Satchel Mouth" became "Satchmo." Although no one can say for sure, it seems this was an error perpetrated by an English music magazine editor who perhaps couldn't read his own notes and referred to Louis as "Satchmo" in an article.

Despite a prodigious early career performing with the likes of Bessie Smith and Joe "King" Oliver, his most famous recordings were made comparatively later in his life. These included: *Mack The Knife* (1956), *Hello, Dolly* (1964) and *What A Wonderful World* (1968).

Louis married four times, the longest to Lucille Wilson his last wife of almost thirty years, and he had no children.

He was a man who cared about his country and his people and who personified the American dream in all of its finest aspects.

He left a legacy of many fine tunes and performances.

Source: https://www.biography.com/people/louis-armstrong-9188912
Photo by William Gottlieb / Redferns)

Mae West:
In A Class All Her Own
(1893-1980)

Born in Brooklyn, New York, in 1893, Mary Jane West entered a world of bustling pushcarts and gas-lit streets. Her bloodline was a mélange, and she boasted of Bavarian, Irish and Jewish ancestry. Her father was a boxer, (Battlin' Joe West) and her mother, who bore a striking resemblance to Lillian Russell in her youth, was a corset and fashion model with a perfect figure.

Mae was the favorite of three children and started her career in vaudeville as *Baby Mae, Performer of Song And Dance*, at the tender age of six. From vaudeville she went on to Broadway, her big break coming in 1928 with the smash hit, *Diamond Lil*. The name came from her father's nickname for her mother, Champagne Til. (Her name was Matilda, and she barely drank more than a few sips of champagne on special occasions.)

Mae West was also a writer, and she chose the name Jane Mast, as a pen name. She wrote on taboo subjects of the day, like lesbianism and free love, and her play, *Sex,* got her into trouble when in 1927 she and the entire cast were arrested and prosecuted on morals charges.

But she was outspoken, daring and no hypocrite. She believed in sexual and racial equality, and was one of the first stars of her day to insist on integrated casts for her productions. She starred in many films with many co-stars, but only one with whom her name is almost always associated: W.C. Fields. They made *My Little Chicadee* together and that was it. Mae didn't care for him at all, and when confronted with his son who wanted to meet her many years later, she simply replied, "I have met one Fields in my lifetime and that is enough."

She died in 1980 at the age of 87.

For the woman who "used to be Snow White but drifted," there will always be many adoring fans.

Source: https://www.biography.com/people/mae-west-9528264
Photo: Michael Ochs Archives / Getty Images

Merle Oberon: Exotic Beauty Personified (1911-1979)

Born Estelle Merle O'Brien Thompson, in Bombay, India, on February 19, 1911, this great star was of mixed Welsh and Indian parentage, a fact she tried to conceal. It is sadly ironic, for it was this blend of nationalities that rendered her an inimitably beautiful amalgam. Early publicity stated that she was born in Tasmania rather than India because Tasmania was considered a classier background than her true half-caste origins. Her father hailed from Britain and her mother from Ceylon (now Sri Lanka).

According to her nephew, Michael Korda, she appeared in nightclubs in Bombay while still in her early teens. She met a wealthy young Englishman and traveled with him to London where she became a star at *The Café de Paris*. She then became the girlfriend of a black American jazz musician named Hutch.

Alexander Korda, a Hungarian Jewish movie mogul, discovered "Queenie" in the tea line of a movie studio. The year was 1933 when he changed her name to Merle Oberon and cast her as Anne Boleyn in *The Private Life of Henry the VIII*. This film has the distinction of being the very first British production ever to be nominated for an Academy Award as Best Picture. Merle Oberon and Alexander Korda married in 1939 and she became the first Lady Korda when he was knighted.

Hollywood beckoned in 1934 after her portrayal of Lady Marguerite Blakeney in *The Scarlet Pimpernel*. She earned an Academy Award nomination for Best Actress in 1935 for her performance in the film, *Dark Angel*. She was a star both in Britain and in The United States. Her most critically acclaimed performance, which was hailed by some critics of the day as "masterful," was as Cathy Linton in *Wuthering Heights* (1939).

During the 1940s she appeared in no less than 15 films, including: *The Lodger* opposite Laird Cregar (1944) and *Berlin Express* (1948). Her final film was *Interval* (1973). She retired soon after and lived quietly until her death from a massive stroke in November of 1979.

She was only 68 years old at the time of her death and maintained her beauty until the very end. She had two children, and her daughter, Francesca, years after her mother's death, commissioned a painting of her mother from an old photograph, instructing the painter to lighten her mother's complexion to hide the fact that she was part Indian.

Unfortunately, some things for some people don't ever change.

Source: https://www.imdb.com/name/nm0643353/bio
Photo: Silver Screen Collection / Getty Images

**Montgomery Clift:
A Great Star
With A Sad Life
(1920-1966)**

Actor, Kevin McCarthy, when speaking of his friend, Montgomery Clift, once said that:"he was a man who had everything and it was all for naught." Blessed with good looks, Edward Montgomery Clift entered the world on October 17, 1920, in Omaha, Nebraska. He was born shortly after a twin sister, Roberta, and he had an older brother named Brooks. The father, William Clift, had been very successful in the banking industry, but lost most of his fortune during the Great Depression of 1929. His mother, Ethel, was born out of wedlock, but raised her children as aristocrats, spending the family funds to locate her supposedly illustrious lineage.

Montgomery Clift was practically a child star, making his first appearance on Broadway in *Fly Away Home* in 1933 at the age of thirteen. He remained in New York for ten years, honing his craft and biding his time until he left for the tinsel and fame of Hollywood. He was an accomplished actor, known for the intensity of his performances. Although he had many relationships with women, he was a homosexual man, who feared that "coming out of the closet" would have permanently ruined his star image.

His film debut was *Red River* in 1948 with John Wayne. He was nominated for several Oscars for: *A Place In The Sun* (1951), *From Here To Eternity* (1953) and *Judgment At Nuremberg* (1961).

By 1950, he had his share of medical problems, and in
fact, had been rejected by the armed forces in World War II for
chronic diarrhea. He became a pill-popping alcoholic, a dangerous
and lethal predisposition. He kept looking for answers, and spent
much money and time on psychiatry.

In 1956 while filming *Raintree County*, he ran his car into a tree
after leaving a party at Elizabeth Taylor's house. It was she who
saved him from choking to death by pulling out two teeth that had
become lodged in his throat. His smashed face was rebuilt and he
managed to come to terms with his estranged father, but pills,
drugs, alcohol and guilt over homosexuality continued to wreak
havoc with his personal life.

When he was asked in an interview shortly before his death how
he felt about his life, his reply was: "I've been knifed." He died
in New York on July 23, 1966, at the age of forty-six.

He left a significant film legacy, and Montgomery Clift
will always live on in the hearts of his many adoring fans.

Source: https://m.imdb.com/name/nm0001050/trivia
Photo via John Kobal Foundation / Getty Images

The Brothers Nicholas: Dancing Dynamos

Fayard (1914-2006) and Harold Nicholas (1920-2000) were famous tap dancing brothers. The children of traveling vaudeville musicians, they performed regularly at the *Cotton Club* in Harlem, dancing their hearts out for many years. Audiences were amazed at the agility and finesse they demonstrated on the dancing floor.

They were both consummate dancers with incredible acrobatic skills. Performers on stage, in films and on television, their vital dancing style was like no one else's. Veteran dancer, Gregory Hines, once said that no duplications of their routines would ever be possible, and if a movie about the famous pair were ever made, they would have to be computer-generated.

Their big break came in 1943 with the film, *Stormy Weather*. The two brothers performed deftly with Fred Astaire, who greatly admired their expertise. The brothers themselves stated publicly that the key to understanding their style of dancing lies in the fact that they danced with their whole bodies and not just their legs and arms. Anyone who doubts this claim has only to watch one of the many films in which they performed.

Their movements and routines actually take one's breath away and seem super-human. For their contributions to the film industry, they have a star on the Hollywood Walk of Fame at 7083 Hollywood Boulevard.

Harold, the younger brother, died first in 2000. His older brother, Fayard, lived to be 91 years of age before dying of natural causes in January of 2006. (Dancing may be good for the health).

The dancing brothers appeared in almost forty films over the span of their gilded careers. To this day, no one can come close to the dazzling magic they created with their golden feet.

Source: https://www.biography.com/people/groups/the-nicholas-brothers
Image Credit: Rich Roll Youtube www.pinterest.eu

Orson Welles:
A Man Beyond His Times
(1915-1985)

He was born in Kenosha, Wisconsin, on May 6, 1915, which was the same day that Babe Ruth hit his very first home run. George Orson Welles was the only son of a well-to-do inventor , who made a fortune inventing a carbide lamp for bicycles, and a beautiful concert pianist who taught him how to play the piano and the violin. In many ways, he was a child prodigy, gifted in the arts of magic, music and painting.

His parents, Richard and Beatrice, introduced their son to worlds far beyond the borders of the American Mid West. His childhood was traumatized, however, by his parents' separation, which occurred when he was only four years of age.

Orson was a cosmopolitan child, traveling around the world with his father after the death of his mother from jaundice when he was nine years of age. When his father's business failed, he became a heavy drinker and died when Orson was fifteen. He became a ward of a family friend, orthopedist, Dr. Maurice Bernstein, who had known him from the time he was 18 months old.

It was Dr. Bernstein who first recognized his creative talents and enrolled him in the Todd School in Woodstock, Illinois, where Orson discovered his passion for the theater.

Following graduation from The Todd School in 1931 and turning down college offers, Welles left for Dublin, paying his way with a small inheritance he had received. There he captivated audiences in a production of *Jew Suss* at the Gate Theatre. By this time, he recognized his love for acting, but his attempts to enter the London and Broadway stages were unsuccessful.

Through recommendations from Thornton Wilder and Alexander Woollcott, he gained entry into Katherine Cornell's road company. He made his Broadway debut in 1934 with his role as Tybalt in *Romeo and Juliet* when was 19 years of age. This performance was pivotal to his career, as it caught the attention of director, John Houseman, who then cast Welles in his *Federal Theatre Project*.

This was a good year for Orson, as within its span, he married, directed his first short and appeared on radio for the first time. This would prove to be a very effective medium for the actor with one of the deepest, most recognizable voices in all of film, radio or television.

All during the 1930s he worked at various radio stations, and he found it difficult to arrive at studios on time for his live shows because of heavy traffic. He found a loophole in the law about not needing to be sick to hire an ambulance, and so he did just that. He instructed drivers to blare their sirens as they traveled throughout New York City so that he could be on time.

The Houseman-Welles partnership was a very important one. In 1937, the 21-year-old actor, who had just finished directing an all-black cast in a version of Macbeth, teamed up with Houseman to form the Mercury Theatre. A highly successful adaptation of

Julius Caesar in contemporary dress with tones of Fascist Italy was its first production.

That same year, along with John Houseman, Welles formed the Mercury Players, and in 1938 the famous radio program meant as a Halloween prank, H.G. Welles *The War of The Worlds,* was broadcast.

It created quite a stir, and many thought it was a real newscast, which was no small tribute to Welles' abilities. The Mercury moved into the realm of radio and began producing a weekly program which ran from 1938 to 1940 as *The Mercury Theatre on the Air* .

His first and most famous film was *Citizen Kane,* which he wrote, starred in and produced in 1941at the tender age of 26. He made many films, the most famous of which included: *The Lady from Shanghai* (1947), which he made with his soon to be ex-wife, Rita Hayworth, *The Third Man* (1949) with Joseph Cotton and *A Touch of Evil* (1958) with Charlton Heston.

He was one of six actors to ever receive an Academy Award nomination for Best Actor for his very first screen appearance.

He was married three times and had three children. Even as a master filmmaker and actor at the peak of his career, Welles maintained his membership in the Magician's Union and regularly practiced sleight-of-hand magic.

He became obese in his 40s, weighing over 350 pounds toward the end of his life. It was said that his average dinner consisted of two steaks cooked rare and a pint of scotch. He was so big that when he dined out, he would often call ahead for a table for six. Restaurant personnel finally caught on when no one else ever showed up at his table, but celebrity has its persuasions and he got away with this ruse often in the last years of his life.

He made a great contribution to the world of film. He considered black and white to be "the actor's best friend," because the medium helped to focus more on facial expressions and feelings than on extraneous color from hair, eyes and wardrobe.

He died of a heart attack on October 10, 1985, leaving a long legacy as a fine filmmaker and actor.

Sources: https://www.biography.com/people/orson-welles-9527363
and https://www.biography.com/filmmaker/orson-welles
Photo by Daniel Farson / Picture Post / Getty Images

Paul Newman:
The Blue-Eyed Legend
(1925-2008)

The son of a successful sporting goods store owner, Paul Leonard Newman entered the world on January 26, 1925, in Shaker Heights, Ohio. His mother was a Hungarian-born Catholic and his father was a Jew of Hungarian and Polish ancestry. He also had a brother named Arthur. Paul was an actor even in grade school, his famous blue eyes enchanting all those who crossed his path. After being discharged from the US Navy in 1946, he enrolled at Kenyon College. After graduation, he spent a year at Yale Drama School.

He soon headed for New York, armed with his blue eyes and a lot of sex appeal. There, he attended the famed New York Actor's Studio. In 1953, he made his first Broadway appearance in *Picnic*, and after that television parts came very easily for him. Warner Brothers offered him a contract, and in 1954 signed him for his first film, *The Silver Chalice*. He himself felt his performance was so bad that he actually took out a full-page ad in a trade paper apologizing to anyone who might have seen the movie.

His next movie, *Somebody Up There Likes Me* (1956), catapulted him to stardom. He portrayed boxer, Rocky Graziano, and the critics praised his outstanding performance. Paul Newman went on to become one of the top box office draws of the 1960s.

Some of his films included: *Exodus* (1960); *The Hustler* (1961); *The Prize* (1963); *Hud* (1963); *Cool Hand Luke* (1967); and *Butch Cassidy and the Sundance Kid* (1969).

Nominated 19 times for an Oscar, he finally won in 1986 for his performance in *The Color of Money*.

He lived with his wife, Joanne Woodward, in Westport, Connecticut, and was the founder of *Newman's Own*, a successful line of food products the proceeds of which go to charity.

He died of cancer in 2008. He was a fine actor and a caring, very generous member of society.

Source: https://www.imdb.com/name/nm0000056/bio
Photo: Mark Kauffman / Time Life Pictures / Getty

**Pearl Bailey:
A Versatile Performer
(1918-1990)**

Born in Virginia on March 29, 1918, Pearly Mae Bailey was the child of Reverend Joseph and Ella Mae Bailey.

Her parents had anticipated a male child and when a girl was born, they nicknamed her "Dickie." Her early life was spent in Washington DC where she received her primary education. As a young girl, she often appeared as a dancer in the Old Howard Theater in downtown Washington. She also worked in vaudeville as both a singer and a dancer.

Pearl was a composer, singer, songwriter and actress all rolled up into one talented package! In the early 1940s, she toured with the Cootie Williams orchestra and later was a featured singer in nightclubs, radio and television.

She made her Broadway debut in *Saint Louis Woman* in 1946. A very versatile performer, Pearl also made many records and scored a hit in 1952 with a song that reached the top ten: *Two to Tango*. She won a Tony Award for her leading role in *Hello, Dolly* in 1968. During the 1970s, she had her own television show and provided the voices for the animations of *Tubby The Tuba* (1976) and Disney's *The Fox and The Hound* (1981).

Pearl Bailey is perhaps best remembered for her memorable performances in *Carmen Jones* as Frankie and as Aunt Hagar opposite Nat King Cole in *St Louis Blues,* the movie biography of composer, W.C. Handy.

Her achievements went far beyond the theatrical. In 1985 at the age of 66, she earned a degree in Theology from Georgetown University. She was awarded a *Presidential Medal of Freedom* on October 17, 1988.

Pearl was married to jazz drummer, Louis Bellson, and had two children. She died in Philadelphia from heart failure in August of 1990 after collapsing at a local hotel.

Source: https://www.imdb.com/name/nm0000056/bio
Photo: Creator: Afro Newspaper / Gado Credit: Getty Images

Ray Milland:
A Fine English Star
(1905-1986)

Reginald Alfred Truscott-Jones was born in Wales on January 3, 1905. Little is known of his very early childhood years. He served three years with the Royal Household Cavalry in London as a guardsman and then entered the British cinema in 1929 when he appeared in *The Plaything*.

Stories abound about his name change, but in his own biography he said to his agent, "I don't really care what you call me. I must keep the initial 'R' because my mother had it engraved on my suitcases. But if you don't come up with something soon, I'm packing these suitcases and going back to the mill lands where I came from."

He found Hollywood (or it found him) in 1930 and for several years afterwards he played mostly second leads. He graduated to a leading man in the mid 1930s, and his charming good looks and debonair manner made him the perfect star for many of the drawing room comedies that were so popular at the time. Although he was always an accomplished performer, little note was made of his talents until 1945 and his memorable portrayal of an alcoholic writer in *The Lost Weekend,* for which he won an Academy Award.

Ray Milland has the distinction of being the only winner of *The Best Actor Award* to have accepted without a single word, opting instead to simply bow his appreciation before casually exiting the stage. He was also the first actor to win an Acting Award at the Cannes Film Festival and an Oscar for the same role (*The Lost Weekend*).

Ray Milland was part of the dynamic Hollywood scene for almost half a century, starting as a novice and working his way up to leading man, competent director and distinguished character actor. Although in his later years he took his share of "schlock parts" to keep busy and pay the bills, his reputation as a fine actor remains untarnished.

He was married to the same woman for 54 years and had two children, a son and a daughter. He died of lung cancer on March 10 1986.

Source: https://www.imdb.com/name/nm0001537/bio
Photo: News photo, Getty Images

Richard Burton:
An Actor's Actor
(1925-1984)

Born November 10, 1925, Richard Walter Jenkins was the son of a Welsh coal miner. He showed promise in acting at an early age and received a scholarship to study the craft at Oxford University. Truly one of the great United Kingdom actors of the post World War II era, Richard made his stage debut in the 1940s. His early appearances were effective but insignificant until producers began to notice his extraordinary talent. In 1952, he got the leading role in *My Cousin, Rachel* opposite Olivia De Havilland.

The reviews were excellent and he made several films at this time including:*The Robe* (1953) and *Alexander the Great* (1956). He also appeared in many stage productions. The late 1950s in the United Kingdom were referred to as "The British New Wave," and Burton was its shining star. Perhaps his most outstanding performance at this time was his role in *Look Back In Anger*, which he made in 1959. He was moving along very nicely and then his life drastically changed in 1962. It was then that he was selected to play Marc Antony in the film, *Cleopatra*, opposite Elizabeth Taylor.

Many consider his most riveting performances to be *Beckett* (1964) and *The Spy Who Came In From The Cold* (1965).His affair with Taylor broke up two marriages, and the couple married and appeared in several movies together over the years, including: *The Sandpiper* (1965), *Who's Afraid of Virginia Woolf?* (1966) and *The Taming of The Shrew* (1967).

In the 1970s, he lost a bit of his golden touch, as quality male roles were going to younger stars. He accepted films of dubious quality just to pay the bills. An avid fan of Shakespeare, he once said, "home is where the books are."

He had a long and formidable career, although it was not long enough for his many adoring fans.

He died in Switzerland at the age of 59 from a cerebral hemorrhage on August 5, 1984.

Source: https://www.biography.com/people/richard-burton-9232503
Photo by John Springer Collection / CORBIS / Corbis via Getty Images

Robert Mitchum:
Bad Boy and Unlikely Hero
(1917-1997)

Born on August 6, 1917, in Bridgeport, Connecticut, this bad boy screen legend had an unlikely start in life. He was of Scottish, Norwegian, Irish and possibly Native-American descent. One of two children, his father was a railroad worker who died in a train accident when he was two years old. His mother and stepfather, who was a British Army major and perhaps the first object of his contempt for authority, raised him and his brother, John.

He was a rebellious and truculent teen, and he spent many of his early years on the open road. At the age of 14, he was charged with vagrancy and sentenced to a Georgia chain gang from which he escaped. Before becoming an actor, he held a variety of odd jobs including one at Lockheed Aircraft, where job stress caused him to suffer from temporary blindness.

He joined an amateur theater company in Long Beach, California, and began to obtain small roles in films. In 1945, his performance in *The Story of GI Joe* earned him an Oscar nomination for *Best Actor* and he became a star very quickly. He was soon seen in many film noir presentations, although he was equally adept in westerns and romantic dramas. He became an icon; a position not at all tarnished and perhaps even enhanced by a 1949 prison term for marijuana usage. He was a tough bad boy and women loved him.

Although he was voted the 61st Greatest Movie Star of all time by *Entertainment Weekly*, in 1970, he turned down the leading role in *Patton* because he believed he would ruin the film.

He was treated for alcoholism at the *Betty Ford Center* in 1984 and died one day before Jimmy Stewart (July 1, 1997). Always the bad boy, he remained with his wife, Dorothy, for sixty years, despite numerous affairs.

He insisted on no memorial service at his funeral, but his ashes were scattered at sea by his wife and neighbor, Jane Russell.

Source: https://www.imdb.com/name/nm0000053/bio
Photo: Getty Images

Robert Taylor:
The Perfect Profile
(1911-1969)

Spangler Arlington Brugh was born on August 4, 1911, in Filley, Nebraska. The son of a country doctor, he came to California in the early 1930s and studied medicine briefly at Pomona College. The handsome, wavy-haired actor, who for a time during his peak rivaled Clark Gable as the screen's top romantic lead, made his film debut in a bit part in *Handy Andy (1934)*. Dubbed "the man with the perfect profile," MGM couldn't help but notice him. They soon offered him a contract and groomed him for stardom.

At first, he made film shorts including the long-running *Crime Does Not Pay* series, but then he moved his way up into the popular "B" pictures of the day such as: *Times Square Lady* And *Murder in the Fleet* (both 1935).

But it was not destined to be MGM Studios that would give Robert Taylor his big break. Loaned out to Universal Studios, he appeared opposite Irene Dunne in *The Magnificent Obsession* (1935) and won the hearts of countless adoring fans (all female, of course).

He married Barbara Stanwyck in 1939 and continued to be immensely popular among female moviegoers. He went on to make other significant films. Some of these included:

Waterloo Bridge opposite Vivien Leigh (1940), *Billy The Kid* (1941), *Johnny Eager* (1941) and *Song of Russia* (1943).

In 1947 he testified before the House of Un-American Activities Committee, providing evidence against Howard Da Silva.

He continued playing leading roles well into the 1950s including *Ivanhoe* (1952), *The Knights of The Round Table* (1953) and *Return of The Gunfighter* (1966).

After a twenty-five year run as a movie star, he tried his hand at television with some success.

Robert Taylor died of lung cancer on June 8, 1969, leaving a rich legacy of film and television appearances.

Source: https://www.imdb.com/name/nm0001791/bio
Photo: Archive Photos, Getty Images

**Rod Steiger:
A Man of Many Talents
(1925-2002)**

Born April 14, 1925, to Lutheran parents in Westhampton, New York, Rodney Stephan Steiger ran away from home at age 16 to join the navy. He served in combat in World War II on destroyers in the South Pacific. After the war, he settled in New Jersey and began to study acting with Lee Strasberg and Elia Kazan at The Actor's Studio. Always possessing the unique ability to suck the viewer into his character, Steiger was a classic method actor. His first break came in 1951 in the film, *Theresa*.

His first leading role came a few years later in the television adaptation of *Marty* in 1953. His breakthrough role was undoubtedly in the classic film, *On The Waterfront* opposite Marlon Brando in 1954.

Known for his diversity, he could play virtually any part and convince any audience that he actually was that personality. He not only had the capacity to look different, he "seeped" the characters he portrayed in a way few actors can.

He was married five times and had two children, one of whom, a daughter, Anna Steiger, is an opera singer. He, too, possessed an operatic voice, but had no ear for keeping in the same key, which rendered his singing voice almost useless.

Of the more than 100 films he appeared in, his personal favorite was *The Pawnbroker* (1964). His riveting portrayal of a Jewish concentration-camp survivor won him an Oscar nomination.

He won a Best Actor Oscar in 1967 for his role as a bigoted sheriff in the film, *In The Heat of the Night*.

He received the Gift of Life Award after speaking out against the social stigma of mental depression from which he suffered for eight years.

He died in Los Angeles on July 9, 2002.

Ruby Keeler:
Canada's Dancing Delight
(1909-1993)

Ethel Hilda Keeler was born on August 25, 1909, in Halifax, Nova Scotia, Canada. Her lineage was Irish Catholic, and when she was three years old, her family moved to New York City. She was one of six children, and although she expressed an interest in dance at a very early age, the family could not afford to give her lessons.

As a child, she attended parochial school on Manhattan's East Side. One day a week a dance teacher would come to the school and teach to interested students. She saw potential in Ruby, and spoke to her mother about taking lessons at her studio. When her mother declined because of a lack of funds, she offered her services free.

In the dance classes she attended, Ruby met another student who told her all about the world of chorus girls. Both girls were thirteen, (three years younger than the legal requirement), but they lied and went to an audition. This led to a part in George M. Cohan's *The Rise of Rosie O'Reilly* (1923), which paid her forty-five dollars a week.

She worked at Texas Guinan's nightclub where she met Al Jolson, whom she began dating. They married in 1928; she was 19 years of age; he was 42. They adopted a son, but the marriage did not go well and the couple divorced in 1940. She found happiness with a second husband, John Homer Lowe, whom she married in 1941. The couple had four children and their marriage ended with his death from cancer in 1969.

In 1933, Ruby was cast in Daryl F. Zanuck's musical, *Forty Second Street*, opposite Dick Powell and Bebe Daniels. Busby Berkeley's lavish choreography made the film an enormous success. Warner Brothers gave her a long-term contract, and cast her in *Gold Diggers of 1933*, and *Dames* (1934). She left show business in 1941, and went on to raise four children. Her two sisters, Helen and Gertrude Keeler, were also actresses. In 1971, she came out of retirement to star in the Broadway revival of *No, No Nanette*, which was directed by Busby Berkeley.

Ruby Keeler was the motion picture industry's very first tap dancing star.

She died of cancer on February 28, 1993, at the age of 83.
She has a Star on the Hollywood Walk of Fame at 6730 Hollywood Boulevard.

Source: https://www.imdb.com/name/nm0444528/bio
Photo: Creator: General Photographic Agency Credit: Getty Images

**Rudolph Valentino:
The Immortal Sheik
(1895-1926)**

Rodolfo Alfonzo Rafaelo Pierre Filibert Gugliemi di Valenta d'Antonguolla (whew!) was born on May 6, 1895, in Castellaneta, Italy, to French and Italian parents. He had an older brother, Alberto, and a younger sister, Maria, both of whom were ignored by their mother who doted instead on her "beautiful baby boy." His father had worked in a traveling circus and then became a veterinarian before marrying his mother.

By the age of eleven, Rodolfo had been expelled from many schools because he was recalcitrant and a bully. He did eventually earn a diploma, and in 1913, armed with a $4,000 inheritance, sailed first to Paris and then to New York.

He learned apache dancing in Paris, but in New York pursued the latest dance craze, the tango, at which he became very proficient. In 1917, he went to Hollywood where he got a small part in *Alimony*. Directors began to cast him as a villain rather than a lover, and he yearned to be a romantic leading man. He became a star when scriptwriter, June Mathis, and director, Rex Ingram, convinced Metro to cast Valentino in the lead role in *The Four Horsemen of The Apocalypse* in 1921. This movie was Metro's first million-dollar production, and it saved the studio from bankruptcy.

Other parts followed, most notably *The Sheik* (1921), *Camille* (1921), *Blood and Sand* (1922) and *Son of The Sheik* in 1926. He married twice in his short lifetime, once to Natasha Rambova and once to Jean Acker in the shortest recorded marriage in history (six hours)! At the time of his death, he was engaged to marry actress, Pola Negri.

There is no question that Valentino almost single-handedly Americanized the Argentine tango. Despite his enormous stardom, his movie career spanned barely six years. Still, he was the among the earliest of male sex symbols of the American cinema. (Harry Houdini was first.)

He died at the age of 31 on August 23, 1926, of blood poisoning caused by a perforated ulcer. Eighty thousand mourners attended his New York funeral, and for many years on the anniversary of his death, a mysterious woman dressed in black was seen laying a wreath of flowers on his grave.

In 1994 Valentino's face was pictured on a 29-cent stamp celebrating the stars of the silent era.

Source: https://www.biography.com/people/rudolph-valentino-9514591
Feature Source: Getty Images

Selena Quintanilla: Death Of A Rose (1971-1995)

Born April 16, 1971, Selena Quintanilla Perez was a talented, Mexican-American singer who left the world far too soon. Her tragic murder in March of 1995 at the age of 23 and at the pinnacle of her success, left an indelible void in the world of Tejano music and in the hearts of her family and many adoring fans. She began singing at the age of nine, and everyone who saw her believed that she had a star quality, a magical glow that would propel her into fame and fortune.

The family experienced more than its share of misfortune: a failing restaurant brought on bankruptcy and life on the streets. In Corpus Christi, Texas, the family made a new start, and through much hard work and effort, Selena recorded her first album in 1984.

Her popularity grew, and because traveling to perform interfered with school, her father pulled her out when she was in the 8th grade. Even though she was not attending classes, Selena earned a high school degree from a correspondence school in Chicago.

In 1986, with the release of her second album, Selena's career began to take off. At the Tejano Music Awards, she won *Female Vocalist of the Year*. In 1988, two more albums were released, and in 1989 she signed with Capitol/EMI Latin label. Her concerts attracted thousands of fans and her own band kept expanding. In

1990, a new guitarist, Chris Perez, joined the band. He and Selena fell in love and married in 1992.

The year, 1990, also brought one shadow upon the scene, but one that would not permeate the light until it was too late. A woman named Yolanda Saldivar approached Selena's father with the idea of starting a fan club for her favorite star. She became the club's president, and wormed her way into the singer's inner circle. But her greed, dishonesty and jealousy were no longer secrets when Selena's family realized that Yolanda had been embezzling money from several family enterprises.

On March 31, 1995, the singer agreed to meet with Yolanda to retrieve paperwork and to fire her. An argument ensued and Yolanda shot Selena once in the back. The singer died from loss of blood a few hours later.

Her death was a tragic outcry on many levels. Even though her music and her spirit lives on in the hearts of those who loved her, her legacy remains a tragic rose, whose petals withered and died long before their time.

Source: https://www.biography.com/people / selena-189149
Image: Getty Images

Shelley Winters: A Different Kind of Diva (1920- 2006)

Born Shirley Schrift in East St. Louis, Illinois, on August 18, 1920, Shelley Winters passed away of natural causes at the age of 85 on January 14, 2006. Never a stunning leading lady, she still held her own against the prettiest stars, and her work was admirable in every film that she ever made. In her heyday, she was a sultry, svelte, blonde leading lady, and her career spanned Broadway, films and television.

Her early acting training was done under the tutelage of the great English actor, Charles Laughton, and she also studied under Lee Strasberg at the Actor's Studio in New York. She was outspoken and didn't care about how other people felt about her opinions, a fact which got her into trouble more than once.

She wrote two kiss-and-tell books, (*Shelley* in 1980 and *Shelley II* in 1989), ruffling more than a few feathers in the film industry.

When she was first starting out in Hollywood, she roomed with none other than Marilyn Monroe. She claimed that it was she who actually taught Marilyn Monroe how to "act" pretty by tilting her head back, keeping her eyes lowered and her mouth partly opened.

Her first big break came in 1947 when she landed a co-starring role with Ronald Coleman in *A Double Life*. She played the mistress and unfortunate victim of the actor-gone-mad.

Many of her films such as: *A Place In The Sun (1951); The Night of The Hunter (1955); The Diary of Anne Frank* (1959) *and Lolita (1962)* remain classics to this day

Vittoria-Gina, her only child from her marriage to Vittorio Gassman, ,survives her.

Source: https://www.imdb.com/name/nm0001859/bio
Photo: Universal Pictures / Archive Photos/Getty Images

Shirley Temple: Child Star Shining (1928-2014)

Shirley Jane Temple was born on April 23, 1928. This most famous child actress of all time hails from Santa Monica, California, and appeared in more than forty films during the 1930s. One of three children, she began her career at the age of three, after a visiting director selected her from a group of other children in a dance class. Her birth certificate was altered, and it was on her twelfth birthday that she discovered she was really thirteen!

She was, even at the tender age of five, a thoroughly professional performer. She was always prepared for "shooting time," her lines memorized and her tap dance steps mastered. In 1935, at the age of seven, she became the very first and youngest child star to receive the "Juvenile Performer" Academy Award. To this very day, her record still stands. She was often paired with actor, James Dunn, as well as Carol Lombard, Gary Cooper, Adolphe Menjou and Arthur Treacher, the kindly butler.

Her abilities as a tap dancer were exceptional. Even at the age of five, she could adapt to the most complex set of dance moves and was teamed often with tap master, Bill "Bojangles" Robinson, who often coached her and helped her develop her technique. She made four films with Robinson: *The Little Colonel (1934)*, *The Littlest Rebel (1935), Rebecca of Sunnybrook Farm (1937)* and *Just Around The Corner (1938)*. When the movies were shown in the many cities of the American South, those scenes where African-American Robinson is seen holding hands with white Temple were edited out!

Shirley Temple became an icon in her own time, which is a tenuous and unusual state of being. Many products were made and sold in her image; such as: dolls dressed in costumes from her movies; dresses, hair-bows; drinking cups and spoons. In addition, several of her songs including: *On The Good Ship Lollipop (1934), Animal Crackers In My Soup* (1935) and *Goodnight My Love* (1936) became popular radio hits.

She was married first to actor, John Agar, when she was seventeen ,and they had one daughter together. They divorced in 1950, and then she married Charles Black, a California businessman. They had two children, a boy and a girl. Shirley Temple Black has received numerous honorary awards and degrees for her work serving humanitarian causes, including the most prestigious Screen Actor's Guild "Lifetime Achievement Award."

She began her diplomatic career in 1969 and served as the US ambassador to both Ghana and Czechoslovakia. In 1972 at the age of 44, she contracted breast cancer, but she survived and lived to the ripe old age of 85, despite being a life-long smoker (which she never did in public).

Source: http://www.shirleytemple.com / biography.html
Photo Source: Wikpedia.com

**Spencer Tracy:
An Actor
To Reckon With
(1900-1967)**

Spencer Bonaventure Tracy entered the world on April 5, 1900 in Milwaukee, Wisconsin. He was one of two sons born to truck salesman, John Edward and Caroline Brown Tracy. He attended Marquette Academy, but left with his friend, Pat O'Brien, to enlist in the Navy at the outbreak of World War I. He remained at the Norfolk Navy yard in Virginia until the end of the war.

He then attended Ripon College where he performed in plays and decided on acting as a career. He went to New York and roomed with his buddy and fellow actor, Pat O'Brien, while both of them attended the Academy of Dramatic Arts. He did summer stock while supporting himself with all types of menial jobs.

His big break came in 1932 when John Ford saw his critically acclaimed performance in the film, *The Last Mile*. He signed Tracy, who was also known as "Spence," up for another film and the actor moved his family to Hollywood. He made sixteen films in three years, and in 1935, signed with MGM. He became the very first actor to ever win back-to-back Oscars for *Captains Courageous* (1937) and *Boys Town* (1938).

He had a brief affair with Loretta Young in the 1930s, but found his true love in an actress with whom he made more than a few films. He and Katherine Hepburn shared a remarkable chemistry that is evident in all of their performances together. Their affair was life-long and began in 1942.

He and his wife, Louise, did not live together, but he never sought a divorce because he was a Catholic.

He died of a heart attack in June of 1967, shortly after what his very last performance in *Guess Who's Coming To Dinner?*

His film legacy is formidable and his performances are as durable today as they were in years past.

Source: https://www.imdb.com / name/nm0000075 / bio
Photo: by ullstein bild via Getty Images

Stewart Granger:
An English Super Star
(1913-1993)

Born on May 6, 1913, in
London, England, James
Lablanche Stewart was
the grandson of actor,
Luigi Lablanche. His real
name was James Leblanche
Stewart, but he was obliged to
change it so that he would not
be confused with the famous
American actor, James
Maitland Stewart. In an
interview he once said that his
off-screen friends always called him "Jimmy."

He made his film debut in 1933 as an extra, but his next film,
The Man In Gray (1943), made him a huge star in Britain almost
overnight. His box office success attracted the powers that be of
Hollywood and he moved there in the early 1950s. He starred in
a number of adventure films, notably *Scaramouche* in 1952 with
Mel Ferrer and *The Prisoner of Zenda* with Deborah Kerr, with
whom he had an extra-marital affair that same year. He was known
to do all of his own stunt work and his dashing manner, tall stature
and theatrical voice made him a natural candidate for he-man roles.

He was best friends with Michael Wilding and also Michael
Powell. When he heard that Powell was looking for a dancer
for *The Red Shoes* (1948), it was he who suggested Moira
Shearer for the part, which made her famous.

Stewart Granger became an American citizen in 1956, the same year he starred with his second wife, Jean Simmons, in the Victorian thriller, *Footsteps in The Fog*.

He married three times and had four children: one by Caroline LeCerf (his last wife) one with Jean Simmons and two, Jaime and Lindsey, with Elspeth March, his first spouse.

During his career, he made more than 60 movies and once admitted that he couldn't stand any of them. In his autobiography, *Sparks Fly Upwards* however, he stated that the 1948 film, *Saraband For Dead Lovers*, which co-starred Joan Greenwood, was one starring role that he did like.

He died of cancer at the age of 80 in Santa Monica on August 16, 1993.

Source: https://www.imdb.com / name/nm0001289 / bio
Photo by Columbia Pictures / Getty Images

Susan Hayward: The Beautiful Brooklyn Babe (1918-1975)

Edythe Marrener was born on June 30, 1918 in the Flatbush section of Brooklyn, New York (where anything can happen, and I ought to know because I was born there myself). Her parents were Irish and Swedish and thus her beautiful red mane and milky complexion. The youngest of three children, she grew up in poverty, in the shadow of an older sister named Florence who was her mother's favorite. Perceived maternal neglect was a life-long, unresolved psychological issue for the beautiful girl who would become the screen legend, Susan Hayward.

After graduating from high school, she studied for a career in fashion design and her good looks landed her many jobs as a photographer's model. She was the sole support of her family in these early years. Her movie career started in 1937 when she was brought to Hollywood after winning a chance for a screen test for the most coveted part at the time, that of Scarlett O'Hara in *Gone With the Wind*. Although she and all the others lost to Vivian Leigh, Edythe did manage to secure extra work and bit parts at Warner Brothers.

After several years of training, she emerged as Susan Hayward and in 1939 signed a contract with Paramount. She was unhappy, however, because the studio insisted on giving her secondary roles, and finally she won her first leading role in *The Fighting Seabees* opposite John Wayne in 1944 while on loan to another studio. Although she made many movies in her short lifetime, her greatest roles were: *I'll Cry Tomorrow* (1955), the story of singer, Lillian Roth and *I Want to Live*, the death row drama about Barbara Graham in 1958 for which she won an Academy Award for Best Actress.

Susan Hayward was a heavy smoker and drinker and was diagnosed with brain cancer in 1972 at the age of 54. She died in March of 1975. There is still a great deal of controversy as to what caused her cancer, as it is alleged that it might have been the result of being exposed to dangerous toxins on location in Utah while making *The Conqueror* in 1956. All of the leading actors, John Wayne, Agnes Morehead, John Hoyt and director, Dick Powell, died of cancer.

Her footprints at Grauman's Chinese Theater are the only ones set in gold dust.

Source: https://www.imdb.com / name/nm0001333 / bio
Photo by Archive Photos / Getty Images

Sydney Greenstreet: A Villain of Stature (1879-1954)

Entering the world on December 27, 1879, in Sandwich, Kent, England, Sydney Greenstreet was one of eight children born to a leather merchant. Little is known of his mother and other siblings, but he left home at age 18 to make his fortune as a tea planter in Ceylon. Drought forced him out of what might have been a lucrative business opportunity, and Sydney returned to England to start anew.

He managed a brewery for a short time and, just as a lark, began to take acting lessons. He was cast as a villain even in his first appearance, which he made in a 1902 production of *Sherlock Holmes*.

He began to appear in many plays, both in England and in the United States. Throughout the 1930s, he was affiliated with the Theater Guild of Alfred Lunt and Lynn Fontaine. At this time, his parts were varied, ranging from Shakespeare to musical comedy. They were numbered, however, for soon he became the cinema's very favorite villain.

He was 62 years of age and weighed nearly 300 pounds in 1941 when he appeared in his first film. He was perfect as white-suited, sinister Kasper Gutman in the classic production of *The Maltese*

Falcon, which co-starred Humphrey Bogart and Peter Lorre. He worked with Lorre in eight more movies. It is truly amazing to note that his entire film career only lasted eight years, and that he suffered with diabetes and Bright's Disease all the way through it. Still, he left a legacy of 24 films! His career ended almost eight decades ago and yet he is still very well remembered and recognized.

In 1949, he retired from the world of film, but had a minor career in radio, starring as the title character on NBC's *The New Adventures of Nero Wolfe* from 1950-1951.

He died at the age of 75 on January 18, 1954, leaving one son, John Odgen Greenstreet who died at the age of 84 in March of 2004.

Source: https://www.biography.com/people/sydney-greenstreet-20702429
Photo by Pictorial Parade / Moviepix / Getty Images

**Thelma Ritter:
One Crack
Character Actress
(1902-1969)**

Thelma Ritter was born
in Brooklyn, New York
on February 14, 1902.
She began acting as a
child in grade school, and
as a teenager performed in
high school plays.

She also appeared in stock
companies after which she trained
as an actress at The American Academy of Dramatic Arts. Her
first movie role, which she got through director, George Seaton,
who was a family friend, was in the film, *Miracle on 34th Street*.
Although she was nominated six times for an Academy Award
during her career, she never received one. She is tied with Deborah
Kerr for the most nominations for a female actor for an acting
award without winning!

Her stage career was lackluster and she left to raise a family,
returning via a career in radio during the 1940s. She found a niche
in this popular medium and appeared regularly on such shows as:
Mr. District Attorney, *Big Town* and *The Aldrich Family*.

Hard-boiled, wisecracking and outspoken, Thelma Ritter was a
fine character actress, who was known for her sense of timing,
unique gravelly voice and small stature. Perhaps her most popular
roles were as James Stewart's nurse in *Rear Window* and Bette
Davis' devoted maid in *All About Eve*. Her films included:

Letter To Three Wives (1949), *Call Northside 77* (1948), *The Mating Season* (1951), *With A Song In My Heart* (1952), *Pickup On South Street* (1953), *Titanic* (1953), *Birdman of Alcatraz* (1962) and *Pillow Talk* (1959) to name more than a few.

She was also a guest on many television series during the 1950s and 1960s including *Wagon Train* and *Alfred Hitchcock Presents*.

She died of a heart attack shortly after appearing on the "Jerry Lewis Show" on February 4, 1969 in New York City. She left a significant film legacy for all of her fans to enjoy for years to come.

Source: https://www.imdb.com / name/nm0728812/bio
Photo by 20th Century-Fox / Getty Images

**Tyrone Power:
One Handsome
Swashbuckler
(1913-1958)**

Born in Cincinnati, Ohio, on May 3, 1913, Tyrone Edmond Power Jr. came from a long line of actors. This very handsome man was the third Tyrone Power of four in an acting dynasty that dated back to the 18th century. His great grandfather was an Irish comedian, his father, Tyrone Power Sr., was a huge star in theater and in films, and his mother (Patia Riaume) was a Shakespearean actress as well as a respected drama coach.

As a child, he was frail and sickly, and his parents took him to California because of the warmer climate. They soon divorced, after which he and his sister, Anne, returned to Ohio with their mother. Tyrone maintained a relationship with his father who encouraged his early dreams of becoming an actor. He appeared in his father's stage production of *The Merchant of Venice* in Chicago, and held him in his arms as he died of a heart attack on the set of a film, a fate that would befall him less than 30 years later.

He got a few small roles in minor films, but steady work in Hollywood was elusive despite his awesome good looks. In 1936, after a screen test, Twentieth Century Fox offered him a contract. He soon catapulted to leading roles, and within a year, he was one of Fox's leading stars. He was not an actor of tremendous caliber or range, and most of his roles were superficial albeit colorful and always displaying his fine face and figure. He joined the US Marines in World War II and was sent to the South Pacific.

After the war, he sought deeper roles and got his best reviews for *Nightmare Alley* (1947) in which he portrayed a con-man. Despite this and his enormous stardom, he still could not land those roles that required real skill and dramatic talent. He worked on stage and also produced films. Perhaps his best performance of the 1950s was in Billy Wilder's *Witness For the Prosecution* (1957).

In Madrid, Spain, on November 15, 1958, during a dueling scene with George Sanders on the set of *Solomon and Sheba*, Tyrone Power collapsed and died of a heart attack before reaching the hospital.

He was only 45 years old when he died and he left three children, all of whom have followed their famous father in the acting profession.

Source: https://www.imdb.com/name/nm0000061/bio
Photo by Silver Screen Collection / Getty Images

**Vincent Price:
The King Of
Grand Guignol
(1911-1993)**

Born in St. Louis, Missouri, on May 27, 1911, Vincent Leonard Price was a man who lived up to his words. He once said, "a man who limits his interests, limits his life." Accomplished actor, gourmet and connoisseur of fine art, he was a highly educated and cultured gentleman.

He traveled throughout Europe and received a degree in Art History from Yale University. An avid art collector, he founded the *Vincent Price Gallery of East Los Angeles College,* which is still in operation. He was married three times and had two children, a boy, Vincent Barrett, and a girl, Victoria.

His first theatrical appearance occurred in 1935 in the Gate Theatre's production of *Chicago*. His, screen debut came in 1938 with the film, *Service de Luxe.* After many minor roles, the most famous of which was as Gene Tierney's playboy fiancé in the thriller, *Laura,* in 1944, he eventually found his niche in low budget horror films. Perhaps the best of the early ones was *The House of Wax,* which was made in 1953. The story centers on a crazed museum curator, who has a sense of realism for his wax figures that more than borders on the homicidal.

Maniacs became his specialty; tortured souls like Roderick Usher in the highly atmospheric *House of Usher (*1960), which was based on a short story by horror master, Edgar Allen Poe. Another Poe story that became a cinematic platform wa : *The Pit and The Pendulum,* which was made in 1961. Seeking new heights of lunacy, Price starred in *The Abominable Dr. Phibe (*1971), who was much worse than his cousin, the snowman with the same moniker . Eventually, he went to England to specialize in these kinds of films because, as he once said in an interview with Johnny Carson on *The Tonight Show*, "Over there, the horror film is more respected as an art form."

The 1970s found him abandoning his career in film and presenting cooking programs for television. With his second wife, Mary Grant, he wrote: *A Treasury of Great Recipes.*

Known to be notoriously superstitious, he once joked that he kept a horseshoe, a crucifix and a mezuzah on his front door. According to Price, when he and friend, Peter Lorre, went to Bela Lugosi's funeral and saw Lugosi dressed in his famous Dracula garb, Lorre said, "Do you think we should drive a stake through his heart, just in case?"

Shortly before his death in October of 1993, he said that one of his most favorite roles was the voice of Professor Ratigan in the Disney feature of 1986, *The Great Mouse Detective.*

Source: https://www.imdb.com / name/nm0000061/bio
Photo by: Universal History Archive / UIG via Getty Images

Walter Matthau:
A Face To Live For
(1920-2000)

Born on October 1, 1920, to a pair of Russian Jewish immigrants, Walter John Matthow grew up poor. His father was a peddler who abandoned the family when Walter was three years old. He lived with his mother, a garment worker, and his older brother, Henry, on the Lower East Side of Manhattan where he attended Seward Park High School. He began acting at the age of eleven, appearing at the Yiddish Theater for 50 cents a performance. He served in the Army during World War II as a radio cryptographer and returned home a sergeant with six battle stars.

His very first Broadway role happened in 1948 when he was hired as an understudy for Rex Harrison (playing an 83-year-old bishop) in *Anne of A Thousand Days*. Fame did not come quickly for him, but it did arrive nevertheless, in 1966 and 1968 respectively, with his roles in *The Fortune Cookie* and *The Odd Couple*.

With fame came the shadow of poor health, as he suffered a serious heart attack due to heavy smoking while filming *The Fortune Cookie*. He did not take good care of himself. In 1993 and 1999, he was hospitalized for pneumonia and other medical problems.

He had a serious addiction to gambling, and once estimated his lifetime losses at $5 million. He married twice and had three children and one stepchild. Passionate about classical music, he often sang pieces by Mozart while working on the sets of movies.

He hated being called a comedic actor even though it was something he did extraordinarily well. Around him, no one was ever sure if he was joking or serious, as he told tall tales often and enjoyed seeing how far he could go with them. He and Jack Lemmon were good friends and appeared in 10 movies together.

He died of a heart attack on July 1, 2000 and Jack Lemmon died almost exactly one year later. Both were poignantly eulogized on the *Larry King Show*.

Source: https://www.imdb.com / name/nm0000527/bio
Photo Source: Pinterest

William Desmond Taylor: A Grand Murder Mystery (1872-1922)

Born in Carlow, Ireland, in 1872, William was the third child of British Army Major Deane-Tanner. The family moved to Dublin where William was educated. He failed the army entrance examination while still in his teens and was forced to leave the family. Much of his early life is unknown, but he did show up in New York around the turn of the last century and found work as a stage actor, engineer and antique dealer.

He entered the silent film industry around 1912 when he obtained his first part in *The Counterfeiter* (1913). That same year, he was in another film, *The Iconoclast,* but was most noted for his performance in *Captain Alvarez* (1914). Also in 1914, he directed *The Awakening,* his first endeavor for Balboa Films. Afterwards, he directed for the cinematic giants of the day including: American Film, Favorite Players, Pallas, Morosco, Fox and Paramount, to name a few.

William Desmond Taylor studied the movie business as both an actor and a director. Some of his films fared poorly, such as *Ben Blair* (1916), while others such as *American Beauty* (1916) were very well received. In July of 1918 at the age of 41, Taylor enlisted in the Canadian Army. He served until the summer of 1919.

After his return from service, he directed the highly acclaimed film, *Ann of Green Gables* (1919).

He resumed his career after World War One. He directed many of the great stars of the day with tremendous success. These included: Dustin Farnum, Constance Talmadge, Mabel Normand and George Beban among others. He was a man of mystery in many ways; he kept very much to himself and was very private about his social affairs. There were rumors of homosexuality, but they were never verified.

His murder on February 1, 1922, was one of the greatest Hollywood scandals of all time. Who killed him and why remains a mystery to this day, only deepened by the passage of time.

Source: https://www.imdb.com / name/nm0853336/
Photo Source: Pinterest

William Holden: Hollywood's Golden Boy (1918-1981)

William Franklin Beedle Jr. was born in Illinois on April 17, 1918. He was the eldest of three sons born to William Franklin Beedle, Sr, an industrial chemist, and Mary Blanche Ball, a teacher. His ancestry was English, and some of his ancestors emigrated to the United States in the 17th century from the area of Lancaster. The family moved

from Illinois to Pasadena when young William was three years of age, and while attending Pasadena Junior College, he became involved in *The Pasadena Playhouse*. It was here where he got his start after a talent scout discovered him in 1937. The following year he made his debut in a film called *Prison Farm.*

His first starring role would come in *Golden Boy (1939)*, which was produced by Columbia Pictures. In the film, he plays a boxer who dreams of being a violinist. Columbia picked up half of his contract and he alternated between Paramount and Columbia studios before serving in The Army Air Corps during World War II, where he acted in training films.

His career soared to new heights with the making of the very successful *Sunset Boulevard* in 1950. Then came *Stalag 17 (1953)* for which he won an Academy Award, *Sabrina (1954)*, *The*

Country Girl (1954), *Love Is a Many Splendored Thing.* (1955) and *The Bridge Over The River Kwai* (1957) .

He was in more than a few bad movies as well; his contract forced him into doing them. He suffered from alcoholism and depression for many years. In 1966 in Italy, he was involved in an alcohol-related driving accident in which the driver of the other car was killed. Holden was charged with vehicular manslaughter and received an eight-month suspended prison sentence. He felt guilty about this incident for the rest of his life.

For years, he had another secret as well. Holden also did undercover work for the CIA, delivering messages to foreign leaders during his travels.

In his later years, he was involved with actress, Stephanie Powers, with whom he shared a loving relationship. He died in November of 1981 when, while drinking, he fell and ht his head against a coffee table in his home in Santa Monica.

He left a legacy of more than seventy films and a career that spanned more than forty years.

Source: https://www.imdb.com / name/nm0000034/bio
Photo by Smith Collection / Gado / Getty Images

Zachary Scott:
The Villain's Villain
(1914-1965)

Born February 24, 1914, in Austin, Texas, Zachary Thomson Scott Jr. was the son of a wealthy surgeon who was a direct descendant of George Washington via his half-sister, Betty, and the famous William Barclay "Bat" Masterson. Zachary at first intended to follow his father's footsteps into medicine ,and he began his studies at The University of Texas. He found himself very attracted to the world of theater and, in a daring move, dropped out of college and signed up on a freighter bound for England. There, he found work in a provincial repertory, and gained self-confidence and skill.

He returned to Texas, married actress, Elaine Anderson, and was soon active in Austin's local theater where he often performed with his wife. One night, Alfred Lunt was in the audience and recommended them both to the producers of New York's Theater Guild. This marked Zachary Scott's entrance onto the Broadway stage where his star rapidly began to shine. Movie mogul, Jack Warner, soon signed him to a contract for the title role in the 1944 film, *The Mask of Dimitrios*. This was the very first time he was cast as a villain, but far from the last. The slender, sinister-looking performer would become synonymous with the word, "cad."

His all-time cad was perhaps the character he portrayed in *Mildred Pierce* (1945) opposite Joan Crawford. The public loved his nasty veneer and he became type cast as a ne'er-do-well and rogue. He did do other types of roles such as in the film, *The Southerner* (1945), but Warner Brothers did not promote him like many of their other stars. His subsequent films were lackluster.

In 1950, his life changed drastically. He almost drowned in a rafting accident (and would have if he hadn't been rescued by fellow actor, John Emory), and he and his wife divorced.

He subsequently rallied from his depression and married actress, Ruth Ford. He re-directed his energies to stage and television, and even though he made a few more films, he never quite reclaimed his former level of stardom.

In 1965, at the too young age of 51, he was stricken and died of a brain tumor.

He left a legacy of more than twenty films.

Source: https://www.imdb.com / name/nm0779923/bio
Photo by Warner Bros. Pictures / Sunset Boulevard / Corbis via Getty Images

Conclusion

Memories are the stuff that life is made of and this collection will hopefully bring some wistful recall to the cinematic days that are no more and the stars that drove the movie industry. Celebrity and fame may be elusive by some definitions, but the names in this biographical collection will live forever in the hearts of their fans.